ONE SURFACE AT A TIME
MOVING BEYOND MEDIOCRE

Nancie Seymour

ISBN 978-1-64349-882-9 (paperback)
ISBN 978-1-64349-883-6 (digital)

Christian Faith Publishing, Inc.
832 Park Avenue
Meadville, PA 16335
www.christianfaithpublishing.com

Printed in the United States of America

Ron and my great kids- Allie, Billy, Shelby, Savannah, and Kevin
My "refrigerator friends" (You know who you are!)
The staff at Sinai Hospital (Kara, Maria, Eileen, & Sophie) who
helped me survive the darkness and brought me hope again.

INTRODUCTION

If you are opening this book, chances are that you, like myself, are experiencing, a life that is not perfect by any stretch of the imagination. It's a life filled with bad choices, weaknesses, fears, wishes, failures, mistakes, good and bad relationships, good days and bad days all rolled up into one.

In the chapters ahead, by the grace of God, you will learn ways to create a better life, one surface at a time. (Yes, I am learning too!)

You will learn to clean out all the cobwebs, pain and blockages, and mistakes of the past to clear the way to a greatly fulfilling life. You'll experience how to improve the present steps and personal faith walk by creating a joyful and content environment around you.

Your future steps will be improved before they ever happen!

One surface at a time...

Chapter 1

Starting Line

The starting line to this marathon race is a place of honesty with yourself. (Yes, I said *marathon*—not a quick start to finish, and you're done!)

There are many areas that are struggled with daily, and you have wished for change numerous times. There have been previous attempts to change and improve these weak areas with no lasting success. (I can't even tell you how many times I have tried to defeat my false god of food—many, many diets.)

Are you willing to go through this time of aggravation and try again—to possibly fail another time?

This attempt is a very long race of endurance and will, lots of training and long days. There will be days when you don't want to run. You're tired, physically and mentally. You don't want to look at results from previous races and acknowledge all the times you didn't come close to winning or to even finishing. In your heart, somewhere deep inside, you know that you have the ability to do this. But are you really willing to go there? Like peeling an onion, are you willing to peel off the outside layers that make you cry along the way to get to that deeper place?

The chapters that follow will help you to straighten your life, one surface at a time. Marathon runners cannot run the big race just by deciding that they are going to run. A good runner runs shorter distances until his or her body is finally ready for the big race.

For me, it's like cleaning my kitchen. It's overwhelming to think of all the big jobs all at once (what is lurking in those containers in the refrigerator?). I tell myself, "One surface at a time." When I finish cleaning out that shelf in the refrigerator, I will move forward to the shelf in the freezer. But the freezer shelf doesn't have to be today. Just focus on the refrigerator shelf.

One surface at a time.

Who are some real friends along the way? Those friends will stand somewhere along the course, give you a drink of water, and cheer you on. They are the friends who truly care about you, know your struggles, and continue to support you.

After you've passed by and they're no longer in sight, these friends will still silently pray for you and cheer. You know, those close friends whom you might not have talked to in a while, and when you finally catch up with them, it feels like you never missed a beat.

These are not friends who will brag to others and say, "My friend is an amazing marathon runner. I'm too busy to actually be present at the race today, but she'll call me later and fill me in."

The real friends are the people whom you can call in the middle of the night, and they would come. They are the people who would drop anything important that they are doing and change plans if you truly needed them. These are the people who may see you before coffee (yes, it isn't pretty!), slippers, and Kleenex-wiping tears.

So if you want to take on this race to improve your life, start with the following points: admit that it's not going to be short or easy, discern who the friends are who will support you and who might bring negativity to your challenges.

One surface at a time.

Pathways in the race will take you in different directions of your life. Filtering through past memories will remind you of the road you took to arrive at the place that you are today. The pathways of the present will help you to understand and improve relationships and struggles that you face every day. The paths of your faith walk will strengthen, uplift, and sustain you in times when you need them the most.

Remember, if you start down the path and it's too overgrown to go through right now, you can travel down a different path. Some areas in life are too overgrown with pain, fear, and resentment to travel through right now. That's okay. Your body will feel stronger and more confident to return to this path when you have the tools that you need to continue through.

Learn ways to clear painful obstructions as you go. One thing's for certain: deciding that you are *all in* to run this race will change your life forever.

One surface at a time.

CHAPTER 2

PAINFUL MEMORIES

Healing some of the pain or bitterness from your past is one of the steps needed to improve your lives, one surface at a time. The goal is not to forget about things or make them disappear. The objective is to make them accessible to think about, without causing severe depression, anger, or resentment.

The past can be like a bad book that can be picked up, read when you choose, and put back down when you desire. Our pasts will not disappear, but how we react can change.

Surroundings that you grew up in or the kind of person you used to be do not have to be the deciding factors as to the person you are today. Maybe growing up was a dark place, where love was not warm and fuzzy.

You make the decision to build or not to build the wall that prevents others from getting in. That self-made wall is built as self-preservation to prevent you from being hurt as you were in the past. Perhaps you had no control over this pain. Maybe as a child you were forced to live with this darkness and pain.

This weight continues to plague you by refreshing your sharp, painful memories. However, with God's guidance, today can be viewed as a fresh, new start. You are not a child anymore. That darkness can only come and control you as far as you give it permission to come. Satan puts jabs into our thinking, thoughts to make us feel worthless, bitter, and dirty.

A wise person made this statement: "Bitterness is like swallowing poison and hoping the other person gets sick."

Ask yourself these questions: What type of person are you today? How do you react to various situations? What adjectives would you use to describe yourself? Do these words describe a person whom you would desire as a friend, treasured in your life? Do dark clouds seem to follow you around? Are you completely at peace and content to remain this way?

Do your answers to these questions shine any uncomfortable light on your inner self? What are some characteristics that you described? *Loving, stubborn, giving, quick to anger, unrelenting, faithful, unpredictable, unforgiving, trustworthy, untrusting, violent at times?*

Christians are not robots. You have choices about how you react to a situation. Perhaps you feel like you are out of control in your emotions due to circumstances of the past. Make a decision today to react to triggers in a healthy way. You may need to get outside help to learn how to react in positive ways if your whole being is screaming with negative feelings and memories.

Look past those feelings of embarrassment and weakness seeking help. In actuality, right now you are facing a giant and are getting your troops in order! Painful memories from the past can affect your reactions to situations in your present life.

To improve the surfaces of your life, meander through your past life. This may be a prickly, painful experience, so just travel through one small surface at a time. Filter out the bad from the good.

Throughout the Bible, Jesus always put stories into familiar ways so not just scholars but ordinary people (like you and me) could understand His teaching. For example, harvesting grain was something the farmers could understand because that was part of their everyday lives, so Jesus spoke often about winnowing and threshing.

> His winnowing fork is in his hand to clear his threshing floor and to gather the wheat into his barn, but he will burn up the chaff with unquenchable fire. (Luke 3:17, NIV)

In crops like oats, rice, wheat, barley, the edible grain kernel grows on plants with a hull (also sometimes called a husk) surrounding it, which cannot be eaten. That hull must be removed before you can eat the grain. Farmers have to do two things before the grain is ready to prepare to eat: loosen the hull (threshing) and get rid of the hull (winnowing).

In some grains, this process is easy because the hull is already loose, very thin, and easy to remove. Farmers would toss this kind of grain from big flat baskets into the air, letting the *chaff* blow away in the wind. This wind-assisted process for separating the wheat from the chaff is called *winnowing*. However, some grains have very thick and hard hulls and are difficult to remove.

This process of harvesting grain is a similar process to the actions needed to improve your life. The past affects the present and the future in both positive and negative ways. Some of the memories from the past are warm and comforting while others are negative or hurtful. Thoughts from your past need to come forward in your mind. You can thresh and winnow the hull of each memory, getting rid of the unneeded chaff.

Some of the hulls on our memories are loose, thin, and easy to remove; but for some memories, the hull is hard and thick and very difficult to remove.

I would suggest, before trying to clean up the past, even one surface at a time, to find a comfortable, warm place. Read Psalm 103:1–5. Slowly read it. Let God's message of truth saturate your thoughts.

> Praise the Lord, my soul; All my inmost being,
> praise his holy name.
> Praise the Lord, my soul, and forget not all his
> benefits—
> Who forgives all your sins and heals all your
> diseases?
> Who redeems your life from the pit? And crowns
> you with love and compassion?
> Who satisfies your desires with good things?
> So that your youth is renewed like the eagle's.

> Because of His loving kindness and tender mercies, God is willing to heal our lives from destruction, whatever is causing the destruction.
> He is willing to satisfy us with good things and renew our youth, like an eagle.
> (Psalm 103:4–5 NIV)

Read these verses again.

God, who can do anything, is willing to heal your life from those things that are causing destruction—with your family, your workplace, and your illness. God is willing to walk hand in hand to that dark place. Your past will be smoothed, but not erased, so the ragged edges won't viciously cut you. As humans, when a situation is viewed as painful or dangerous, instinct kicks in to fight or take flight.

If there are memories that are hard to hull, you may have deeply buried them. These memories may not immediately come to the forefront of your mind. You may not realize how these memories numerously and negatively connect to your present-day life. Those hidden memories may rear their ugly heads as reactions of anger, resentment, and even abuse to others.

Did someone hurt you in the past? We live in a world of hurt. Even on a good day, there are so many negative things: on the news, in the newspaper, on the radio, and even in own homes, neighborhoods, and churches. Any of these negative events or comments can trigger many unwanted feelings or events from the past.

These levels of pain may range from horrific abuse or neglect to hurt feelings from a friend. Everyone's experience is unique. Every day, different issues appear for each of us to deal with and face.

Yet, no matter how different we are, one thing remains constant in every person: every person innately desires to feel needed, cherished, loved, and cared for.

You need to bring those negative feelings to the forefront. Bring these feelings into the light. No longer will they have any power over you. You will not have forgotten these memories, but no longer will they paralyze you with dread and fear.

CHAPTER 3

DO I REALLY MATTER?

A conflict occurs. The conflict could entail an aggravation, a miscommunication, a "messy" event, like dishes left unclean in the sink or on the table. The conflict occurs, and a heated discussion unfolds. The perpetrator might not even be present at the time. When angry, does a familiar accelerating speed take over your body? Dishes get washed and put away faster. Vacuums move at a record speed. Loads of laundry fly into the washing machine. Even our feet walk much faster when we are angry.

The anger subsides. Next, the negative thoughts start pounding in your heads. Are you truly important? Do you really matter? Do you mean something to anyone? Does anyone even notice the time and hard work you always put in to maintain this family, this job, and this life?

Eventually, after the frustrating and aggravating moments pass away, those cutting thoughts dissipate, and a happier picture appears in the distance. Others do need and love us, even though they don't verbalize it. (They are just put on this earth to make us crazy!)

But for some, these questions never go away. The feeling of stability and love is nonexistent. That "not needed" and "unloved" feeling lingers year after year.

The moment *neglect* starts for many children is the moment that parents realize that a child is coming into this world. Some children come into this world not as treasured, long-awaited joys but as unwanted surprises. They do not outgrow their parents' feelings of "unplanned and unwanted." This concept causes blood pressure to rise. There are a large number of families who would do anything to have a child, to cherish and love, and physically can't birth children on their own.

The domino effect continues the pattern. Children who felt neglected grow up to be adults having children. Their children will feel neglected also, and the pattern continues. The parents have no base of warm, adoring environments. Humans have a tendency to continue living in environments which are familiar, even if they are not happy, warm environments.

The year is 2013.

273,105 babies were born to women ages 15–19
89 percent of teenage parents are unmarried
86,000 teens aged 15–17 gave birth in 2012
Nearly 1,700 teens aged 15–17 give birth every week
About 77 percent of teenage pregnancies are unplanned
Only 50 percent of teen mothers age 15–19 earn a high school diploma
Only 38 percent of teen mothers age 15–17 earn a high school diploma
One and a half percent of women getting pregnant as a teenager have a college degree by thirty years old.
80 percent of unmarried teen mothers end up on welfare
50 percent of teen mothers go on welfare within the first year
22 percent of daughters of teen mothers become teen mothers also

The majority of the adult-life span is modeled after lives experienced as children.

And so the pattern of neglect continues on.

Some children experience the feelings of not being "accepted" and "unloved" after they reach school age. They feel neglected by teachers or authority figures for not protecting or assisting them while being bullied. Being bullied causes bad memories of feelings of neglect, abandonment, and rejection. This cowardly act is used to puff up the person who is bullying. Unfortunately, the presence of bullying can be found every day in our society.

Bullies do have groups of friends. They are not low on the social spectrum, as many believe. They are, however, low on the empathy scale. It does not bother them to watch, or to cause, others to be hurt or controlled.

Why then do people bully others? Various reasons differ from person to person. A bully may have experienced bullying himself by family members or others. The territory is familiar. Lasting reactions from experiencing bullying resound in present lives. Victims of bullying often do not learn how to filter their own anger in healthy ways. There are feelings of distrust, need to be in control, needing feeling of power.

Bullies often target those who are different from their group. A bully will pick out their targets based on a specific reason. Maybe the reason concerns sexuality, race, disability, or lack of interest in a certain thing like sports. They may physically or verbally abuse someone in front of others. The reason for bullying that person may not be spoken aloud, but reasons are clearly obvious to others. Bullies benefit from their actions in ways such as receiving lunch money or gaining social recognition.

Bullying doesn't just happen to young people in schools. Bullies may not outgrow this urge to overpower others. This controlling action may also be experienced in the workplace or at home. The women or children residing in a rescue facility will portray firsthand incidences of how a bully became violent when their power and control felt threatened.

Frequently, in company offices, adult staff members are verbally bullied. The bullies are usually in the popular, outgoing crowd. Social statuses are very important to them. They initiate bullying others to show off to others their strength and control.

The introverted and nonconfrontational team players are the probable targets for bullies. Posing a threat of obtaining a higher standing causes bullies try to shut them down. Work bullies are openly critical, speaking harshly and purposely, excluding others from conversations. Bullies may take credit for others' work, seeking to be viewed as overly confident and in control. Bullies at work tend to pick on people who are quiet and lack confidence.

Improving assertiveness and self-confidence skills educate victims in ways to be excluded as targets of verbal bullying. Stand up for yourself. Don't let yourself appear to be an easy target. If you choose to be silent and not to act, there is nothing to keep this bullying from continuing.

Bullying has to be nipped in the bud to bring a stop to this treatment. Oprah Winfrey, a much- respected role-model, gave the reminder that others will treat you how you *teach* them to treat you. You are the one who makes it clear to others what treatment is acceptable or not tolerated.

Be professional and set limits. The bully will back down. The trick is to hide anger, fear, and hurt feelings. Demand respect calmly and rationally (takes practice, easier said than done at first!).

However, make a note: if this is a spouse or family member physically bullying or abusing, outside help may be needed to make the abuse stop.

Victims of bullying may experience memories and feelings from those interactions. The act of being bullied as a young person may have ended. Perhaps the bullying stopped because of an environment or location change. If this is the case, there has been no healthy closure to these incidents. Present lives are affected by the negative memories under the surface. The correlation may not even be realized and identified.

In what ways can bad memories from being bullied rear their ugly heads again in present lives? Someone has taken control and manipulated another. Victims feel weak and powerless.

Character traits and social statures were questioned, causing self -esteem to be drastically lowered. Victims' brains have been programed with negative feelings of not being good enough and not having the ability to succeed.

Imagine a workplace with a group of employees standing in a group, laughing about something. Your neck gets hot and prickly. Thoughts go through your brain that this conversation must be about you. Coworkers may be having an innocent conversation, but those old feelings of exclusion rear up. The warm flow of embarrassment and humiliation appears again.

Bullying means someone is controlling and manipulating. Victims are forced to feel weak and powerless. Character traits and social stature have been questioned. Emotions range from pain, frustration, anger, and bitterness.

These hurtful feelings have to be brought into the conscience and into the light to change the impact. These looming dark feelings are not the magnified drastic monsters that they always appeared to be. You will not be governed by the past.

Bullying is not new to the modern world. King Saul was a bully. He harassed and chased David relentlessly. First Samuel 18:6–12 talks about Saul being jealous of David. He was insecure and felt extremely intimidated by David. For no reason (except for being jealous), King Saul sought out to bring harm to David.

David was bullied and harassed and chased by Saul for seven chapters in the Bible. That did not affect the great king that David turned out to be.

So how can this surface of bullying and attacking feelings be wiped clean to move forward? The wish to clear out bad memories and negative feelings from our past lives so those hurtful feelings of bullying do not resurface.

The "new" you, with God traveling along, will shine with the confidence that God has promised with guidance and protection—one surface at a time.

Look to God and the Bible for guidance and help to bring many encouraging thoughts to counteract the false thoughts.

Pick one of the following verses each day. Read it several times during your days to remind yourself that it is through God's peace and courage that you can be the person that you want to be, not created by the bad memories from a giant Goliath in the past.

> Fear not, for I am with you; be not dismayed, for I am your God; I will strengthen you, I will help you, I will uphold you with my righteous right hand. (Isaiah 41:10)

> Cast your burden on the LORD, and he will sustain you; he will never permit the righteous to be moved. (Psalm 55:22)

> Come to me, all who labor and are heavy laden, and I will give you rest. Take my yoke upon you, and learn from me, for I am gentle and lowly in heart, and you will find rest for your souls. (Matthew 11:28–29)

> Peace I leave with you; my peace I give to you. Not as the world gives do I give to you. Let not your hearts be troubled, neither let them be afraid. (John 14:27)

> And let the peace of Christ rule in your hearts, to which indeed you were called in one body. And be thankful. (Colossians 3:15)

Words of wisdom from some well-known biblical scholars remind us how God will help you through this path of painful memories. You will come out much healthier and happier on the other side.

> God will not be absent when His people are on trial; he will stand in court as their advocate, to plead on their behalf. (Charles Haddon Spurgeon)

You are valuable because you exist. Not because of what you do or what you have done, but simply because you are. (Max Lucado)

Be assured, if you walk with Him and look to Him, and expect help from Him, He will never fail you. (George Mueller)

The stars may fall, but God's promises will stand and be fulfilled. (J. I. Packer)

You hold the steering wheels of your life. God blessed you with free options and the right to make choices. It is always your choice in life to stay where you are or to venture ahead with God's blessing. The past is a memory. It can only control your present and future as much as you allow.

Just like David, after his hardships with Saul, a fulfilling life lies waiting ahead.

Greatness awaits if—and it's a big *if*—you choose to let the past stay in the past and not allow it to control you today.

CHAPTER 4

SELF-ABUSE

Unlike bullying or abuse by another person, the abuse that is put upon oneself often goes unnoticed. Blocking this invisible abuse is essential if you want a more peaceful and stable present.

Years ago, the infamous toy the Rubik's Cube was very popular. The goal of the toy was to try to manipulate different colored squares and ultimately end up with all of the same color on each side of the cube. Building a better life is similar. Aspects of your life have to be turned over with many adjustments and attempts. Some succeed, and some do not.

You're probably thinking this chapter is not going to be for you because you are certainly blessed. You certainly never allow yourself to do without. This type of unseen abuse is dangerous because often it is unrecognized and ignored. Identifying and then modifying actions will help to build stronger and more prosperous lives.

Self-criticism/high standards are very familiar nouns listed on my own report card. Does your report card look similar?

I am definitely my own worst critic. Like manipulating a Rubik's cube, I continuously examine steps of the project that I am working on. Negative thoughts pop up randomly into my head such as components of the work needing to be fixed because of imperfections. The project at hand may refer to a semi-important job at work or a simple task of a household project. How many times are explanations given as to why the work didn't turn out exactly as hoped?

Aside from self-criticism, these imperfections may not even get noticed. Others see a great product. The abnormalities in our work always glare out at us, even before the work's completion. Our standards for ourselves are always higher than the standards for others. Aerotechnical engineers, whose errors may result in tragedy or death, should be held to this level of perfection. However, looking at our works in the grand picture of life, our standards of perfection should be lowered. Yet we allow no room for any errors for ourselves.

Teach yourself to observe work as glasses half full instead of half empty. Be aware of these negative tendencies. For every criticism found, make a conscious effort to counter the negative thought with a positive. Over time, the mind will be trained to see the positive along with the negatives. The moment of triumph is when it is realized that the positive aspects outweigh the negative criticisms. Positive self-esteem begins in childhood. However, views of one's self can be modified during adulthood when positive thoughts are filtered in.

> The Lord your God is in your midst, a Warrior who saves. He will rejoice over you with joy; He will be quiet in His love (making no mention of your past sins), He will rejoice over you with shouts of joy. (Zephaniah 3:17, AMP)

God doesn't *just* love us. He treasures us and adores each of us. Treasuring something means you can turn something every angle and adore it. God adores us, complete with our dirtiness from sins, fogginess within our faiths, stains and all. Our Maker cherishes us. Cherishes!

> For I know that nothing can keep us from the love of God. Death cannot! Life cannot! Angels cannot! Leaders cannot! Any other power cannot! Hard things now or in the future cannot! The world above or the world below cannot! Any other living thing cannot keep us away from the

love of God, which is ours, through Christ Jesus, our Lord. (Romans 8:38–39, NLV)

Harried time is another abuse that we subject ourselves to. The familiar adjective used in describing this abuse is *busy*. Busyness is not an abuse if we are filling our time with fulfilling two things: furthering God's kingdom, combining our busy times with touching people for Him, and savoring the blessings that God has given by combining happiness with busyness.

You may be shaking your head and thinking, that is an impossibility. You need to bring a paycheck home. Your work is a stressful, busy place, and the children require all of your time. You're forever running here and there, and you don't have time or energy to further God's kingdom!

Everyone has experienced the feeling of being a gerbil in a wheel, running in circles every day. From within, false perceptions are made, showing no meaningful progress. From the outside, people are watching and acknowledging our reactions, interactions, and demeanor. Furthering God's kingdom doesn't mean performing like great evangelists (thank goodness!). During those busy moments when we are forced to run on the gerbil wheel, we can still be furthering God's kingdom.

I planted the seed, Apollo's watered it, but God has been making it grow. So neither the one who plants nor the one who waters is anything, but only God, who makes things grow. (Corinthians 3:6–9, NIV)

The one who plants and the one who waters have one purpose, and they will each be rewarded according to their own labor. For we are coworkers in God's service, you are God's field, God's building.

The majority of people are not the amazing planters or evangelists like the late Billy Graham. But whether happening interactions with teachers, coaches, carpool moms, bosses, fellow employees, or

Uber drivers, you can be the Christians that water! God promises that each will be rewarded for his labors.

Be aware of your surroundings. Be mindful of someone going through a hard time. Interactions can be as simple as pats on shoulder for illnesses in a family. Store-bought cookies can be gifts for someone losing a spouse. A scribbled note can communicate thoughts and prayers for another. God uses Christians as vessels of comfort while improving His kingdom. How can busy times possibly be combined with true and peaceful happiness? Is that even possible?

God know you so well that He has your name written on His hand. He knows your every move. David reminds us of this a lot. God knows about all about the busyness. He gave it to you. Your work is your God-given task.

> You discern my going out and my lying down;
> You are familiar with all my ways.
>
> Before a word is on my tongue You, Lord, know it completely. You hem me in behind and before, and you lay your hand upon me. (Psalm 139:3–5, NIV)

> I have seen the God-given task with which the sons of men are to be occupied. He has made everything beautiful in its time. Also, He has put eternity in their hearts, except that no one can find out the work that God does from beginning to end. I know that nothing is better for them than to rejoice, and to do good in their lives, and also that every man should eat and drink and enjoy the good of all his labor—it is the gift of God. (Ecclesiastes 3:10–13, NKJV)

God tells you to eat, drink, and enjoy your life, including busyness and hard work. Every day, in the midst of the busyness, stop and look around and thank the Lord for the amazing gifts. Those gifts surround you and are used every day. Most people just power-walk past them so fast there is no time allowed to take notice.

Treasuring yourself is another avenue to steer away from self-abuse. When a precious, delicate, collectible antique is owned, it is touched gingerly and kept in a safe place (it is hard to view our own self as a delicate collectible). You truly are precious to God. Take measures in treasuring yourself!

The problem with society is that the perfect body portrayed in the magazines is about half the average size. It's easy to look in a mirror and not like what we see.

Enjoy all parts that God has blessed you with. Learn how to keep enjoyment focused on thankfulness to Him. Don't let blessings take control and lure you away from the focus on Him. God wants you to enjoy His gifts, showing thankfulness to Him always.

Weight loss has become a big industry, both for medical purposes and emotional reasons. Put it in perspective. Losing weight, gaining weight, feeling guilt should not take your focus off God. Invite Him to walk through the journey with you.

Take your focus off yourself and stop being so critical. Focus on all the blessings that God provides for you every day and thank Him for all He has done. Then enjoy those blessings with a carefree and guilt-free heart.

CHAPTER 5

NORTH, SOUTH, EAST, OR WEST?

Being unsure of the direction in life leads to insecurity, frustration, and hopelessness. Comfort and peace comes from knowing the correct direction to be heading. God is directing you in where you are meant to be. He gave you the key piece to your purpose by sending Jesus Christ to carry your load of sins to the cross. It is because of His sacrifice that you are able to approach God at all. When you die, you will be given your last direction toward flowing peace, unbridled happiness, and rest for your weary self. No matter how this fact is twisted or turned, it remains a win-win situation!

Looking at everyday lives, the pictures are not always filled with sunshine and roses. Living in a hectic, and often chaotic, world, the gerbil ball takes over, going round and round and not getting anywhere. Hard work and perception of the lack of progress lead to frustration and even resentment. There seems to be no end in sight.

The bad ride can have a misleading security to it. Even though it is not an optimum situation, it's a familiar situation. Often, staying in painful but familiar situations is easier than venturing out and away.

A poor economy causes people to be unemployed. Bringing home a paycheck is a necessity. The bills pile up, and there seems no end in sight. There are distant dreams of getting out of a stressful work environment; however, the economic factors keep one from leaving.

Job security is not a given. In many companies every year, each employee has to have a one-on-one evaluation with the executive to determine whether the employment will be continued for another year. It is saddening to frequently see this happen within our professional sports teams. A favorite baseball or football player goes through a slump and gets moved down to a minor league or traded to another team. That constant feeling of insecurity of facing the unknown is a heavy weight to carry around.

Frustration also abounds when a person feels defeat or dissatisfaction. The perspective is that they're giving 150 percent, and something is preventing them from succeeding. Technology changes so fast that it's hard to keep up with the modifications. Younger employees are more up-to-date and can keep up with changing demands. Insecurity and frustration over time lead to hopelessness. Hopeless people do not prosper at home or in a workplace. They feel defeated before the day even starts.

Do you feel tired and defeated in the morning, even before your feet hit the floor? If this describes the beginnings of your days, you are not alone. The fact that you are reading this book shows that there is still hope flickering within. Learning how to build and maintain a more meaningful and productive life is not just a quick fix. You will be directed toward a more carefree life, without all the exhaustion.

So aside from quitting your present life and moving into Siberia, in what ways can you spruce up your present life?

Feeling insecure builds up and spills over into other aspects of your life. What is causing that insecurity? What are the trigger points? Close your eyes and imagine an insecure time. Now imagine opening a brown bag. Stuff the negative thoughts about being useless, unneeded, slow, disliked, or not respected down in the bag. Tightly close the bag and store it in an imaginary drawer. It's not possible to make the negative feelings disappear as if they were never real. In reality, those insecure feelings of the past existed, but they don't gauge who you really are today and what could happen in your life tomorrow.

Many days are filled with frustrations that range from small irritations to long-term irritations. Today is the perfect example of morning irritations for me and working up a sweat, even through the cool morning air. The sequence of morning irritations included the puppy knocking his food bowl, a floor to be riddled with little dog-food grenades, pouring a bowl of cereal only to find out that there is no milk, a coffee cup accidentally tipped over, and attempting to clean up the spill, realizing that the cardboard paper-towel roll is completely empty. This is the frustrating final straw to the start of the day.

Everyone has experienced these types of mornings. They're not the kind of mornings where one would call the pastor in tears, but definitely, things have not gotten off to a smooth start. These are the days when you need to make the conscious effort of watching yourself from the outside, like an *I Love Lucy* show and laugh.

"God, I'm glad You are present to watch this comedy act this morning!"

On a very rainy day, while driving with my eighty-year-old mother, she gave me some great advice. This particular day had been one of those frustrating days. Mom instructed me to pull the car over and stop. She said, "Don't let something bad ruin your day. Dance in the rain." She directed me to get out of the car, and two grown women danced in the rain!

If you are set in the direction that you are supposed to be heading, through God, you are able to tolerate the aggravations and challenges.

God shows the importance of following the direction of life through the salmon, whose life follows the template of following a direction. (If you haven't realized it yet, God blessed me with child-like thoughts. I'm similar to the people in the Bible. I need to have things explained to me in simple, everyday ways! If you are a scholarly-type person, I am sorry.) Salmon are born upstream in a river. The mother lays her eggs in shallow gravel. She covers them with a little bit more gravel after the father salmon fertilizes the eggs.

After birth, the baby salmon or "fry" float and swim downstream. The "fry" are a favorite delicacy to bass, trout, and some birds. They must learn to avoid predators who will happily gobble up the small salmon. Instinctively, between birth and two years old, the salmon will swim upstream to their feeding ground. This chosen feeding ground could be two hundred miles away toward the ocean. This area will remain their feeding ground for several years.

Salmon are very small and weak on this trek. God provides insects and plankton for food along the way. As Christians, we must trust that God will keep His promises and provide for us while we are following His direction.

> Look at the birds of the air; they do not sow or reap or store away in barns, and yet your heavenly Father feeds them. (Matthew 6:26, NIV)

Are we not much more valuable than they?

After salmon reach the ocean, they may travel up to one thousand miles to Alaska or far out in the ocean to feed on fish, squid, eels, and shrimp (traveling and eating sounds like a good plan to me!). After living in the ocean for years, the salmon are bigger and stronger. Instinctively, they must return to the stream where they were hatched to lay their eggs and produce offspring. Before traveling upstream to hatching grounds, salmon spend their time eating to get stronger and bigger.

Christians also need to build strength to survive and succeed. We need to build and empower our faiths. Unfortunately, many wrongly think like the salmon: that eating a lot will make us stronger! Being present in the Word of God is our source of power, not food! It's like a shot of strength in our arms. This rush of strength comes forth while stepping forward in God's direction for His plan for our lives.

Salmon swim through strong fast-moving currents day and night to get upstream to their birthplaces. Probably, at this moment, those salmon that traveled one thousand miles to eat are thinking they wish they had picked a closer feeding ground!

Salmon experts think that they use their sense of smell to return to their hatching place. Not long after they "spawn" or "procreate," the salmon's life cycle is finished, and they die. The cycle continues from salmon generation to generation.

Never forget where you came from and all the challenges that it took to get to where you are today. You need to follow that inner drive, like the salmon, that pushes you to follow God's plan. Difficult times, distractions, and challenges will be experienced along the way. Press on, with the promise that forging on will bring fulfilling lives to fruition. Your present environments are just stopping points on the long journey of your life.

Many good or bad factors affect the present and contribute to the person who you are today. Never forget the starting place on the journey toward what God has promised. We must return to the same place of creation.

CHAPTER 6

SEE THE FOREST THROUGH THE TREES

Rush, rush, rush or "got to make the donuts," the old commercial used to say. There are so many moments that are missed because of hurried traveling through life at such a great speed.

On January 12, 2002, Joshua Bell, world-renowned concert violinist, participated in an experiment for the *Washington Post*. Bell played for free for forty-five minutes on a violin worth three and a half million dollars at a subway station. He had just played in a packed concert the night before where people had to wait in a lottery line to purchase a ticket. Now, playing in the subway, on the very next day, over a thousand people passed by him. Only seven stopped to listen to him play, including a three-year-old boy. Only one person recognized him. Twenty-seven gave money, most of them on the run, for a total of thirty-two dollars and change.

Are you hurrying past something worthwhile nearby? Important glimpses of beauty are being overlooked in our rushes and routines. Valuable connections with others and opportunities are missed because we rush by.

God's plan for your life doesn't solely include your participation in allotted "God-service" times. Your world is filled with people with whom valuable acknowledgement and connection would be a benefit. People of every age and walk of life carry with them memories, valuable lessons learned, and new insights. Take a moment to notice uplifting and lighthearted glimpses. Stop in the rush to notice them. No moment can be too minute or useless.

Frequently missed moments could include waving to a neighbor picking up the newspaper at the same time you do, the smiling teenager at the register at the coffee stop, a mailman who waves hello as he passes, the warm receptionist at a doctor's office, teachers, bus drivers, greeters at Wal-Mart, a friend's unexpected phone call, or doormen, secretaries, or custodians in an office building. Many possible connections are encountered, yet distractions pull the other way.

Daily encounters with people are affected a lot by amplified or untrue feelings. Do judgments ever stem from clothes or appearance? Are a person's emotions ever misjudged because of the perception of facial expressions? Misperception causes negativity and covers over any beauty that might be noticed.

Unfortunately, negativity does not always accidentally happen because of misconceptions. Troubling, bad-luck times cause a rush of very valid negativity. There are no misconceptions here! Perhaps an employer hires a younger, more advanced employee, or a business crashing causes unemployment. Our minds scream out that there is no beauty here. Anger, fear, frustration, and bitterness make it very difficult to see beyond.

However, by leaning on God's promises, beauty can be seen in spite of the crisis. This too shall pass. Paul speaks of hardships in 2 Corinthians. He was beaten three times with rods, stoned once, shipwrecked three times, and thrown in jail (our hardships cannot possibly compare to his hardships, right?). Paul held on to the promises and still saw the good.

> That is why, for Christ's sake, I delight in weaknesses, in insults, in hardships, in persecutions, in difficulties. For when I am weak, then I am strong. (2 Corinthians 12:10, NIV)

Crisis after crisis will come. Christians are not excused from facing them, nor will the reasons behind these challenging times be clearly understood. Trusting in God's plan will carry you through the trials. The key to success is to listen closely for God's voice and then to walk in His plan, even through the hardships.

A familiar song says, "I have decided to follow Jesus. No turning back, no turning back." These words were the last words of a man in India in the middle of the nineteenth century, whose wife and himself were executed for not denouncing their faiths. How can it be at all possible to see beauty in such dark times? God's promise that it is all going to be okay is the only light that illuminates times as dark as this.

> "For I know the plans I have for you," declares the Lord, "plans to prosper you and not to harm you, plans to give you hope and a future." (Jeremiah 29:11, NIV)

That verse is so familiar. Yet if you are like myself, you try to go your own ways, with your desires in life. You don't listen to that voice of God pointing you to where you should go. Your own ideas prompt you because you are smart enough and strong enough to follow your own whims. Finally, after umpteen tries, you tell God that you're sorry. Sometimes it takes almost a hit in the head with a hammer before the obvious is seen. God has been trying to tell you all along to follow His plan and not yours. Through all the extraneous distractions, you and I can't see the forest through the trees!

You move through life and go through the motions that are familiar. But sometimes God nudges you to do something different. Humans are prone to overthink a situation and not travel on instinct. Maybe you are feeling a nudge from God but aren't positive. In later chapters, you will learn how to ask God for clarification about nudges on big issues. But for now, start to depend on God-given instincts.

WWJD (What would Jesus do?) was a slogan that showed up on bracelets, T-shirts, posters, and necklaces. Every decision made should follow that question. Make decisions on basic Christian truths and not on what the world prompts.

Another reason that forest can't be seen through the trees is that human beings are about as self-centered as they come. Our eyes focus on our lives, our worlds, our emotions, ourselves. Perhaps you may be arguing quietly under your breath with me right now about how big of a heart you have and your empathy overflowing for others.

Well, if that is the case, make mental notes for a whole day. Keep a running count of how many times you are purposefully thinking of others and how many decisions or thoughts are because of your own desires. You will shake your head at the end of the day wondering how you ever got so selfish!

Content means quietly satisfied and happy. Overall, you may be happy with your life, partner, education, or work. But because of the selfish nature, many beautiful moments are missed due to longing for bigger, better things. Feelings of entitlement, pride, need of recognition are the trees blocking our sight.

Often, the grass always seems greener on the other side of the trees. Society pushes that bigger is better. Manufacturers strive to sell products so the environment is filled with dissatisfied, disgruntled people with the feeling that they deserve to experience better things. The blessings for happiness and a wholesome life are already present! They don't have to be purchased or updated constantly.

So what is the remedy?

Be mindful of those people or things around you. Take a breath and listen. Even while in the middle of swirling problems or decisions, stop and listen. You may be able to hear a violin.

CHAPTER 7

M-I-S-S-I-S-S-I-P-P-I (RIVERS OF LIFE)

B esides knowing how to spell the well-known name, what are some facts that you know about a river?

Rivers always flow downhill. Most rivers begin high up in the mountains, where snow from the winter is melting. Glaciers melt and start a river flowing. Rivers always add to life, have moving currents, and are constantly changing.

God has given free choice to make every decision. Life choices are similar to entering a river's current. The first choice is whether to enter the current in the first place. Participating in this experience is a free choice. The challenges will be there. The decision to venture out or to stay on the safe shoreline to watch is completely your decision to make.

The next decision is whether to allow yourself to be swept in the direction and current of God's will. Opening ourselves to respect and follow Him will fill us with His power. However, traveling on God's path, accompanied with conflicts will impede the journey, and hardships will come. Selfish decisions will leave you breathless and exhausted.

Your choice of direction and destination should be fighting against the current of sin and poor choices. Society, friends, and selfish natures will try to pull you into overlooking sinful things and moving with the crowd.

God will always give you a choice as to how to react. Just like with the current of the river, it's very hard and exhausting to make a stand and swim against what everyone else is promoting. But along with that worn-down feeling comes a pat on the shoulder from God, for the good choices!

Rivers are life-giving to those creatures around or within them. Moving in the current through God will bring life. Your life will be meaningful and alive in Him!

God's holy river has many other similarities to our world around us. If the decision is made to get in the river of God's holiness and to follow the pull of God's current, you need to be mindful of things in the environment around you.

Ezekiel's vision describes God's river:

> The man brought me back to the entrance to the temple, and I saw water coming out from under the threshold of the temple toward the east (for the temple faced east). The water was coming down from under the south side of the temple, south of the altar. He then brought me out through the north gate and led me around the outside to the outer gate facing east, and the water was trickling from the south side. As the man went eastward with a measuring line in his hand, he measured off a thousand cubits and then led me through water that was ankle-deep. He measured off another thousand cubits and led me through water that was knee-deep. He measured off another thousand and led me through water that was up to the waist. He measured off another thousand, but now it was a river that I could not cross, because the water had risen and was deep enough to swim in—a river that no one could cross. He asked me, "Son of man, do you see this?" (Ezekiel 47:1–6)

Many Bible scholars and ministers think that this vision represents the river mentioned in the Bible. Could it be the river in heaven?

I am not a Bible scholar. My mind thinks at a childlike level, as you well know by now in reading this book! I don't disagree with the scholars; it's just hard to wrap my head around their highly profound thoughts in my little brain!

Think about your own childhood. Your parents never permitted you to wander aimlessly near a body of water. You had the same restrictions on your own small children about roaming freely near water. How many photographs are taken of a small child, holding hands or in the arms of a loved one, by the ocean's edge?

Wading in shallow water with feet on firm land was the next secession. Obtaining more experience and more confidence, the depth grows deeper and deeper. Swimming under still water becomes successful. Eventually, challenges such as swimming and jumping into waves become enjoyable.

Christian lives are the same way. Starting out, there is little knowledge or understanding of God's ways. Our Christian walk starts from God, who created us in His temple. God entrusted us to our parents, who were our caregivers and advocates. At first, we only knew a little bit of God's world, trusting our parents to teach and lead us in very shallow water.

As childhood progressed, you were permitted to step out into water that was a little deeper. You ventured out a little more from your guides' safe hands. You reached a point in your life that your decisions were your own. Hopefully, adult children will still return to "special" people occasionally for advice and love!

This gentle road is a lot like the walk with Jesus Christ. Faith walks are not journeys where age matters. Even an adult just finding Christ for the first time can't be tossed into deep water and be expected to swim.

Everyone travels on their own different stretch of faith. Living through Christ can feel natural for those raised by Christian families from the start. Others are surviving a difficult life and just finding out the truth about our God. Perhaps someone was leading an evil life, and the light of God turned that life around.

New believers are like small children. They can only move ahead with a person of respect, teaching and protecting them as they wade through shallow water. New believers need a wiser Christian to help them to be aware of dangerous waters ahead.

The river of God's holiness flows through your lives, your families, your churches, and your workplaces. How you choose to experience God's holy river, if you experience it at all, is your choice to make. There are a multitude of plants and animals within that same river.

The river in Ezekiel's vision started at the south side of the temple. The journey of following God's plan also begins with God at His temple.

Look at the river around as a whole. Humans tend to lean on the pride of self-sufficiency and independence. Are you similar to myself, too often caring for my own self and not relying on others for needs? (I like other people; I just do not *need* them!)

The clear picture, which is often foggy and undefined, is that actions and interactions of those around you help to shape the people that you are. Rivers are life-giving, and every feature impacts everything else.

The power in the current causes banks to be transformed so rivers are constantly changing. The landscapes change around them. Erosion wears away land because of the steady pressure as the water goes past. That moving water also takes materials, like plants and soil, downstream to new locations. New streams may be formed as the current pushes the water farther and farther.

The majority of people are frightened by the unfamiliarity of change. The feeling of not seeing a final and finished product is unsettling. Changes can be positive or negative. As a Christian, your life can change because of God's nudging. Perhaps His will is for you to take on a new project or spread your faith out to others.

These nudges could be simple additions, like singing in a choir or visiting church members who are homebound. Sometimes changes could be major decisions such as a different job or moving to a new place.

A few are guided to give up comforts of home and move to foreign territories. The preferable life is to be consistent and without change. Change causes worry and anxiety.

Peter speaks of these anxieties:

> Humble yourselves, therefore, under God's mighty hand, that He may lift you up in due time. Cast all your anxiety on Him because he cares for you. (1 Peter 5:6–7, NIV)

Joyce Meyers says worrying is like a rocking chair; it's always in motion but doesn't get anywhere. We must consciously turn our concerns over to God. Casting your care doesn't mean being irresponsible. God won't do for you what you can do for yourself. You do what you're able to do, and then trust God to do the rest.

When humbling yourself and asking for His help, He releases His power in those situations. It's only then that life can be truly fulfilling.

If God is nudging you into a change, and the fear and anxiety is mounting up, what should be done immediately? *Pray*. God won't lead any into the rapid current to drown. Pray for clarity. Clarity will show that this is God's will, and He will provide for any needs, beyond what you can take care of yourself.

There are areas that we clutch close to our heart, especially where money is concerned. God may be nudging in this area, but often it is ignored or overlooked. Jesus clearly tells us what to expect if we choose obedience in this area.

> Bring all the tithes (the tenth) into the storehouse, so that there may be food in My house, and test Me now in this," says the Lord of hosts, "if I will not open for you the windows of heaven and pour out for you [so great] a blessing until there is no more room to receive it. (Malachi 3:10, AMP)

If you are truly walking in God's will and bringing your tithes to God, you will see the results. He promises that blessings will overflow.

Praying for clarity about a situation means also praying for clarity about yourself. Before entering the current to a new situation, are your heart and actions showing your loyalty to God?

> Do not be anxious about anything, but in every situation, by prayer and petition with thanksgiving, present your requests to God. And the peace of God, which transcends all understanding, will guard your hearts and your minds in Christ Jesus (Philippians 4:6–7, NIV).

Often this passage is read combined with some special "gift" that God will bless you with. Clarity about a situation can be your gift. God promises that His peace will guard your hearts and minds.

Change is always going to be uncomfortable for most of us, even when feeling the involvement of God's hand. Faithfully following a change under God's direction is like riding a roller coaster. There are going to be ups and downs, lots of fears and anticipation; but as Christians know, the hills will come to an end. When arriving at the destination, you will feel exhilarated for making the decision to ride.

God never changes. The currents of your lives change the surroundings. Whether flowing with God's will or against, God *never* changes. God's character *never* changes. Many verses in the Bible attest to this.

> Jesus Christ is the same yesterday and today and forever. (Hebrews 13:8, NIV)

> Every good and perfect gift is from above, coming down from the Father of the heavenly lights, who does not change like shifting shadows. (James 1:17, NIV)

Keep reminding yourself of God's unchanging nature when feeling apprehensive about a direction that God is nudging you to go. God's character never changes. The only thing about God that might change is His mind.

In the Bible, there are instances where God planned on destruction of some groups of people because of their evil ways. Heartfelt prayers changed His mind. The Israelites almost blew it for themselves, but Moses saved their lives by talking to God. Moses sought the favor of the Lord, his God.

"Lord," he said, "why should Your anger burn against Your people, whom You brought out of Egypt with great power and a mighty hand? Why should the Egyptians say, 'It was with evil intent that he brought them out, to kill them in the mountains and to wipe them off the face of the earth'?"

Then the Lord relented and did not bring on His people the disaster He had threatened.

Jonah was also threatened with disaster. God told Jonah to warn the people of Nineveh that they would be destroyed in forty days because of their evil living. The king of Nineveh believed Jonah. He told his people to clean up their acts and repent.

> But let people and animals be covered with sackcloth. Let everyone call urgently on God. Let them give up their evil ways and their violence. Who knows? God may yet relent and with compassion turn from his fierce anger so that we will not perish.
>
> When God saw what they did and how they turned from their evil ways, He relented and did not bring on them the destruction he had threatened. (Jonah 3:8–10, NIV)

The bottom line is this: God's answer key, the Bible, teaches the following truths. Your need should be to do your very best to follow God's will and avoid evil. By doing this, God will lead you and build you up, not destroy you. God's character *never* changes, although your circumstances and environments may change.

God has a plan for you. He already has prepared the destination where you will end up. So once you make the decision to go into the "current" to follow His will, you need to make decisions based on His will.

Along the way, there are actions and projects to take on. These "acts" are not needed to be able to enter the final destination—heaven—but they are, in fact, needed. Christians, made in God's image, love Him and want to have qualities like Him.

> For it is by grace you have been saved, through faith—and this is not from yourselves, it is the gift of God— not by works, so that no one can boast. For we are God's handiwork, created in Christ Jesus to do good works, which God prepared in advance for us to do. (Ephesians 2:8–10, NIV)

> What good is it, my brothers and sisters, if someone claims to have faith but has no deeds? Can such faith save them? Suppose a brother or a sister is without clothes and daily food. If one of you says to them, "Go in peace; keep warm and well fed," but does nothing about their physical needs, what good is it? In the same way, faith by itself, if it is not accompanied by action, is dead.
>
> But someone will say, "You have faith; I have deeds."
>
> Show me your faith without deeds, and I will show you my faith by my deeds. You believe that there is one God. Good! Even the demons believe that—and shudder. (James 2:14–19, NIV)

Christians will do good deeds not because they have to but because if someone truly knows the truth about Jesus Christ, they will strive to be like Him. A Christian can't help letting the love within reach out to show other people.

If you feel like God is nudging you, your first step is to clarify whether or not this action/move is part of God's will and not our will. Pray to God for the clarity and humility.

> God, I pray for clear understanding of this action that I am thinking about. I know that many times I am thinking about my own desires and how I will be acknowledged or respected by following through with this act. Please, Lord, forgive me for any prideful thoughts. If this action is truly Your will, please let me feel Your affirmation about it. Everything that comes from this action, please let it be done all to Your Glory and not my own. In Jesus's name, amen.

That answer will help you to know which direction in the river to attempt to follow. If it's sinful or leads to sin, then strength is needed to swim against the current. God will provide the wisdom and necessary components to lead you in this endeavor. You will hear His voice in many ways when you are seeking direction for His will.

Your vision will become clearer in affirmation of the right road or warning of the wrong road.

CHAPTER 8

SATAN-THE WRECKING MACHINE

Don't talk to strangers. That helpful command from parents was inbred into our souls early in times with warnings about hot stoves and cars in the street.

Satan is a dangerous stranger. Learning to recognize Satan when you see him is the most useful defense in warfare with him. If you were introduced to an enemy clearly, you would take all precautions not to be tricked or misled. But Satan is the father of lies and misconceptions. He uses many different means to question faith and God's goodness. Sadly enough, he tricks and misleads before it is ever identified as his doing. It's not realized that he is working evil until it's already in motion.

> Those who see you stare at you, they ponder your fate: "Is this the man who shook the earth and made kingdoms tremble, who shook kingdoms?" (Isaiah 14:16)

Someday Satan is going to be visible, and his future will be questioned. He will be looked upon, and the question will be asked, "Is this really him?" The impression of him was that he was this powerful entity with all of this power! He will be seen as the sad "want-to-be" who ruined his amazing life in heaven with an all-powerful God. Is this really him? He seemed much bigger.

Satan's greatest desire is to cause interference to keep someone from getting closer to God. What kind of avenues does Satan use to try to block our steps of godly actions?

He uses three predominant factors in his evil schemes: people, emotions, and distraction.

Satan is often looked upon as the "bad side" of a scale where God is the equal "good side." As much as he wishes to be, Satan is *not* equal to God. The book of Job makes it very clear that Satan had to ask permission from God before he caused any bad things to happen to Job.

> Jesus said to the disciple Peter: "Simon, Simon, Satan has asked to sift you as wheat. But I have prayed for you, Simon that your faith may not fail. And when you have turned back, strengthen your brothers." (Luke 22:31–32)

> "Does Job fear God for nothing?" Satan replied. "Have you not put a hedge around him and his household and everything he has? You have blessed the work of his hands, so that his flocks and herds are spread throughout the land. But now stretch out your hand and strike everything he has, and he will surely curse you to your face." (Job 1:10)

> The Lord said to Satan, "Very well, then, everything he has is in your power, but on the man himself do not lay a finger." Then Satan went out from the presence of the Lord. (Job 1:9–12, NIV)

God has provided all the armor needed to protect us from these attacks from Satan. It's like a raging battlefield. Christians, as soldiers of God, are given free choice. They can confront the enemy, wearing nothing but an undershirt, and then choose to give up when tattered and massacred. The other option is to be prepared, wearing the protective armor that God has provided, being patient, taking the blows, and waiting until the enemy is defeated in the end. The end of this story has already been written with Satan defeated, so that makes enduring the pain more bearable.

Rattling faith is what Satan does best. Satan doesn't put a lot of negative energy into non-Christians because he doesn't have to. Their eyes are already blinded, and they are not actively working for God yet. (I say "yet" because none of us, even Satan, can see God's plan for the future direction of a person's heart.)

God gives warnings about Satan in His book. Satan is "the father of all lies" (John 8:44, NIV).

"The thief comes only to steal and kill and destroy" (John 10:10, NIV).

What is Satan's desire? His desire is to stop Christians from being useful in sharing God's message of salvation with others.

What are some roadblocks and attacks that the father of lies utilizes to work through Christians?

Satan is a leader of deception and false implications using people. Playing on areas valuable and meaningful to the victim is his favorite. Weaving deceit and misconstrued feelings through people are two areas through which he utilizes to master his talent. This evil deceit is usually viewed merely as conflict with another person. The underlying motive is not realized. No hidden agendas are apparent. After falling for his trickery, you are caught in his web. Conflict usually leads to anger, frustration, bitterness, or hard feelings. You don't even realize that is Satan bringing on the bad situation, and it could have been avoided altogether.

The problem is not that God doesn't provide guidance and tools needed to identify and avoid these evil attempts to sabotage Christians. The problem lies with Christians acting as teenagers do with parents and not following their wisdom and guidance. God provides the information. Christians just need to put the solutions into action.

> For our struggle is not against flesh and blood,
> but against the rulers, against the authorities,
> against the powers of this dark world and against
> the spiritual forces of evil in the heavenly realms.
> (Ephesians 6:12)

How does Satan catch entangle people in this evil web?

Fear is an emotion that Satan uses frequently. Peter was an example of a very faithful person who fell into Satan's trap with fear.

Matthew 14:22–33 and Luke 22:61–62 tell how Peter denied Jesus three times, leading him to feelings of failure and guilt. Why would something like that happen to someone as loyal as Peter? What understanding can you gain to learn and prevent Satan from causing such anguish in your life?

Peter's personality displayed a lot of outgoing and quickly visible traits. On any day, Peter might be described as headstrong, self-confident, impulsive, unexpected, with no planning ahead. He was always rushing in headfirst, frequently emotional, hotheaded, could have violent tendencies when angry. He devotedly loved his friends, especially Jesus, and would protect them no matter what. The downfall of his passionate personality was that he always acted too quickly without thinking things through.

John MacArthur calls Peter "the apostle with the foot-shaped mouth" because he was always sticking his foot in his mouth. He blurted out and charged ahead without weighing his options.

How many of these characteristics do you see in yourself from time to time? Hmmm.

Why would Peter deny knowing Jesus when obviously Jesus meant so much to him? As a human being, his first urge was to protect himself. He was not prepared to face the shame and beatings that Jesus was facing. He was scared—He knew Jesus's life was in danger, so his life would also be in danger.

Peter denied knowing Jesus to a servant girl who was a relative of the servant whose ear he had just cut off. What do you think she would do if she verified that he was the same man who cut off her relative's ear? It's human nature to do whatever we can do to remain safe.

Earlier, in the gospels of Matthew and Mark, both replay Jesus's conversation with His disciples that soon He was going to suffer die and be raised from the dead.

Peter didn't want to believe this. Being outspoken Peter, he began to rebuke Jesus for having such a negative mind-set. Can't you just hear him saying "How do you know this, Jesus? Stop being so negative. Why would you even think these awful thoughts?" After Peter rebuked Him, Jesus replied, "Get behind me, Satan. You do not have in mind the things of God, but of man" (Mark 8:33, NIV).

Human emotions or struggles entangle us. Anger is felt toward people. Jesus clearly sees Satan's handiwork through the muddled messes that human beings are able to see. Sadly enough, on the other side of the coin, maybe you or I have permitted Satan an opening to allow his handiwork to come through our voices or actions. Be aware of Satan's tactics and ways to avoid them. He attacks in areas of confidence and self-sufficiency. Because protective guards are not up, you are vulnerable, and it's easy to fall victim to his evil schemes.

Fear shakes up confidence and strength. Bravery was Peter's strong point. He took great pride in defending his friends. If Satan succeeds at questioning or inflating failures in these strong areas, disappointment will follow.

Three hundred and sixty-five times in Bible, God says not to be afraid. Satan used fear to get this burly take-charge person Peter to deny Jesus.

Peter faced fear of humiliation, persecution, and death by being one of Jesus's disciples. Satan also knew that Peter would be seriously wounded by the two things that meant most to him: loyalty and bravery. A man with tattered pride can't help but question his purpose and usefulness. Peter's spirit was crushed with these negative feelings and failures. What was the final outcome? Jesus forgave Peter for his sin of cowardliness after His resurrection. Peter, as a faithful servant after the resurrection, went on to play a very big part in creating new churches in Acts.

Peter's failure is an example of never giving up, or giving in, to something you are afraid of. Negative questioning appears often. Was there failure? Were desired outcomes not accomplished? Are you truly important? Do you matter to someone? Maybe a challenge seems impossible, and quitting the fight seems the easy way or only way out.

Don't give up. Don't give up. Don't ever give up. God will never stop until His plans are accomplished.

Think before speaking. (Yes, I am still on the "try, try, and try again" spectrum here!)

Think of specific questions to filter your topic of conversation *before* it exits your mouth. What is my motivation for saying this? What is the desired outcome?

If struggling with impulsive, reckless personality traits is probable, pray to God to grant you a few minutes of mulling something over before commenting. Avoid the possibility of acting as a vessel for Satan.

It's never too late to be forgiven and receive a "do-over" from God. Satan likes to remind Christians over and over about the wrong mistakes committed. The sins seem huge and irreversible. However, God is definite that if you are truly sorry for what you've done, He will never think it's too late to offer forgiveness.

Once again, the Bible holds all of the answers. No matter how awful the sin, true repentance leads to forgiveness and clean slate. The black sin will be forgiven and erased.

Peter's life teaches that God uses ordinary people to be unlikely heroes throughout Bible. Peter was a fisherman from Galilee. Thankfully, you don't have to be Bible scholars or evangelists like Billy Graham to do great things for Christ.

God is calling you and me, the "ordinary people," to be "unlikely heroes" in this short time we are given on earth. So ask yourself this one final question:

Are you willing to keep your eyes on Jesus, saying, "Yes, I do know Jesus," even when you are afraid in whatever challenge you are facing? Or are you going to allow your life to be paralyzed with fear and regrets?

Satan tends to use people whom you love and respect the most to hurt you the most. Words can be a strong weapon. Loved ones can be insensitive, and many times the comments cut right to the bone.

Families and close friends know so much that they know where the weakest points are.

Satan either manipulates people who intentionally choose to be mean to get their points across, or naive people who don't think things through. Naive people don't realize how much their words are causing hurt feelings or bitterness. Some people seem to have a gift for saying the wrong thing at the wrong time and hurting people. They may not even mean to cause harm and are just trying to get their own point across. Hurt feelings are not intentional.

Satan causes other people's actions to inflict great deal of pain as well (I'm finding that I really don't like this dude!). Hateful and hurtful actions can attack, even while kindness and lovingness are being demonstrated by the other person. This harsh treatment is not deserved or provoked. Again, when these actions come from close friends or family, the damage seems all the more substantial.

Satan is the father of lies. He deceives people into actions that will betray, destroy trust, and shatter your heart. God provided protection against the sinful attacks of Satan. The strong armor of God will work and can be worn at any time to revoke Satan. However, the armor can only work if it is used.

> Stand firm then, with the belt of truth buckled around your waist, with the breastplate of righteousness in place, and with your feet fitted with the readiness that comes from the gospel of peace. In addition to all this, take up the shield of faith, with which you can extinguish all the flaming arrows of the evil one. Take the helmet of salvation and the sword of the Spirit, which is the word of God. (Ephesians 6:14–17, NIV)

The belt of truth represents truth spoken by God over you (directly confronts Satan's lies). The belt is a reminder that no lie of Satan will survive. God's truth provides strength.

The breastplate of righteousness protects against guilt or shame. No matter how far a person has fallen in sin, God has already won the battle. God views Christians as righteous and redeemed.

The feet fitted with the readiness from the gospel of peace provides comfort, knowing that no matter what circumstances are happening or how awful they seem, God takes care of Christians. Share this news with others. Be ready to follow God's will, whatever He asks of you.

The shield of faith extinguishes all of Satan's flaming arrows and allows Christians to stand ground in his attacks.

> "No weapon forged against you will prevail, and you will refute every tongue that accuses you. This is the heritage of the servants of the Lord, and this is their vindication from me," declares the Lord. (Isaiah 54:17)

The helmet of salvation relates the truth about how sinful Christians truly are. Jesus saves in spite of what was deserved. Sins are no longer counted against a Christian if forgiveness is requested. Because of Jesus's forgiveness, those who believe in Him will never truly die. They will be blessed to live eternally in paradise.

The sword of the Spirit is the Word of God. The Bible is the treasure map with the answers to every possible question or challenge. As a good father does, God wants to prepare His children for the challenges that lie ahead. He wants to be a trusted *hands-on* Father who provides for all needs and desires. He is faithful and just.

Instructions to help Satan to be recognized when he visits by utilizing the protective shield that God provides are laid out in the Bible.

God grants all Christians to have free choice. It's your decision to hurt internally for a very long time, letting the pain control your future. The other choice is to realize what Satan is trying to accomplish, thwart his evil attempts, and move past his damaging jags.

Remember, Satan's desire is to stop Christians from being useful in God's work of sharing His message of salvation with others. But the choice is always yours. You do not have to curtail to Satan's desire at all. The steps will always be your choices to make.

Satan also uses many events to discourage faith. Some of his attempts could include unanswered prayers, tragedy, grief, discouragement, or failures.

Hearing about a miracle happening to another is always uplifting. Teaching about trusting in God's promises starts very early on. God will not let you down. But hello! I am human! I think I deserve to be a recipient of God's work sometimes too! So how does Satan use God's silence? God's answer to prayers may be a yes, a no, or a maybe and not now. He may seem silent as part of a bigger plan.

Satan uses these seemingly unanswered prayers to dissuade remembering God's promises and turn the focus onto belief in Satan's lies. "See? God isn't listening to you. He obviously doesn't have time to answer your prayers. You are not *that* important." These unanswered prayers put questions and doubt about faith in self and the promises of God. Why are these sincere prayers not being answered? The feelings of unimportance and value seep in. Obviously, these prayers are not worth much in God's eyes. Self-esteem plummets, and many questions above levels of faith arise.

The blame game within starts for whatever was prayed for and not received. Maybe this is a punishment. An action toward a mother is the reason a daughter's pregnancy won't come. Lies and lies and more lies. Satan is the father of lies!

Using emotions is another avenue that Satan frequently uses to sabotage us and stop Christians dead in their tracks from doing God's works. Satan uses people to orchestrate anger and bitterness. This does not promote an ideal creative, healthy, and active Christian atmosphere!

Fear is an emotion that acts as a pendulum between feeling paralyzed and feeling angry with God. Someone dies unexpectedly, and the grief and helpless emotions boil over. Perhaps you have experienced grief over a sudden death of a loved one. The world is heavy and dark with no light in sight. I remember comforting a good friend who lost her husband suddenly at a very young age. Through her well of tears, she wondered aloud how she would survive the very long life that loomed in front of her with three young children.

Another mom lost her teenage son in a car wreck. The anger and resentment at God took over her Christian heart. She stopped going to church and being involved in anything. Many years later, she was still very angry with God for permitting this tragedy to happen in her life.

A job is lost, bills cannot be paid, and the house filled with children might go into foreclosure. Satan uses these feelings of an unfair life to paralyze Christians from surrounding themselves with God's promises and peace. At times, even devout Christians experience anger while feeling that life is very unfair. At whom are we angry? God.

Distraction is another avenue that the subtle, lethal, misleading enemy uses to deter someone's faith walk. Distraction can put a sudden stop to the grand accomplishments that a Christian is in the process of accomplishing to God's glory. Satan convinces, both consciously and unconsciously, that whatever this distraction is, it's completion is very important.

One distraction leads to another and another, and pretty soon the *grand accomplishment for God* has slithered away uncompleted. How many times do you glance at your watch and wonder where the time has gone? Satan, the father of lies, has succeeded in his stealthy mission to distract you.

The story of Nehemiah is a perfect example of Satan's distraction techniques. Nehemiah was called by God to rebuild the walls of Jerusalem. It was when they were nearly finished building that Nehemiah was tempted with distraction. (Of course, Nehemiah didn't fall for it and stayed on course—unlike myself, the queen of distraction!)

> When word came to Sanballat, Tobiah, Geshem
> the Arab and the rest of our enemies that I had
> rebuilt the wall and not a gap was left in it—
> though up to that time I had not set the doors
> in the gates- Sanballat and Geshem sent me this

message: "Come, let us meet together in one of the villages on the plain of Ono." But they were scheming to harm me; so I sent messengers to them with this reply: "I am carrying on a great project and cannot go down. Why should the work stop while I leave it and go down to you?" Four times they sent me the same message, and each time I gave them the same answer. (Nehemiah 6:1-4)

Nehemiah was busy doing the work God had called him to do. He said over and over that he was not to be distracted from his work.

Imagine how irritated Satan would be if every time he tried to cause a distraction from some meaningful work, he got the same answer: "I am carrying on a great project and cannot go down."

How can you tell if the distraction is a work of Satan or a momentary pause directly from God Himself? The first step in dodging Satan's attack of distraction is gaining familiarity with how he works. Satan causes interference. Realizing that he attempts to distract a lot helps you to avoid naively getting swept away into his swift current of deception.

The next step is to ask God for clarity about the situation. "Please, God, if this is a distraction meant to derail me from time spent with You or a work that I am trying to accomplish for You, please make it clear to me. Clear my path so that I can clearly see the way I should go."

Sometimes God will mercifully remove the distraction so your decision is easy. Other times, He will give you clarity to the situation so you will realize that you are indeed being distracted by Satan. After God sheds light on the distraction, He often watches to see what actions you'll take to move forward past the distraction.

Remember, God will not tempt or distract you with something that is not His will. While He is guiding and inspiring, there is a feeling of excitement that feels different from human excitement. It's a deep, meaningful excitement. If you listen very closely, you can hear the angels cheering for you off in the distance!

Whatever action or project within God's plan will initiate attacks from Satan. Don't be scared off, but just expect this resistance from Satan. He does not want any Christian to perform an action for God that will show others how powerful and almighty God is!

Satan will try to sabotage this action in many ways to try to stop any forward motion. One wish is that every example of distraction, God would hold up His hand and give a loud warning. But as usual, God provides wisdom within His Word to give all the answers. The next phase is God watching to see whether His armor or Bible's answer key are used to make a stand against Satan. Following the answer key naturally and frequently would initiate the same response as Nehemiah: "I am carrying on a great project and cannot go down." God allows Satan to try to use these blocks to halt the work for Him. God *allows* this. Satan is not an equal with God. He has to get permission to lay grenades and blockades in your path. But God has provided the tools to protect us against the attacks. Identifying Satan's ploys and making a firm stand is the right way to handle his evil antics.

The battle has already been won. All you have to do to win is believe and show up!

CHAPTER 9

RELATIONSHIPS

Who are you when no one is around? Knowing yourself truthfully and honestly to start with is the only way to change gears and get yourself moving to a more productive life.

Outward images often mask a lot of who resides inside. Appearing to be organized, attentive to detail (my husband calls it being "anal"), caring, thoughtful comes naturally. However, feelings of insecurity, jealousy, or fear are rarely talked about, even with close friends or family.

In this chapter, you will look at some negative characteristics closely and honestly (except me, I have no negative characteristics! LOL).

If you truly wish for a healthier and more meaningful life, instead of making excuses, acknowledge your personality traits. God will shed a new light on personality traits if you ask Him. He will show you avenues either to turn very few negative traits into something worthwhile, or the need to tweak or erase this trait forever. By putting a more positive spin on natural *attributes*, you will indeed improve your present—one surface at a time.

Think about all the characteristics that make you the unique person who you are. God has a grand purpose for you. He created you, and you are His masterpiece that He will guide to completion.

Too Judgmental and Opinionated

Remember, you promised to be honest with yourselves in your soul-searching (yes, I spent some harried time in this chapter as well!).

The characteristics of being judgmental or too opinionated are probably the characteristics where the majority of people, if admitting to this characteristic at all, will reply, "That's just how I am. I was made this way." Having opinions or being judgmental are not bad qualities to have. Christians, however, need to make sure that there is no mightier-than-thou tone attached. God is the only one who is righteous enough to bring judgment on a person. Somehow human beings have a way of lifting themselves up to a higher level than others.

Our judgments are based on what we see, hear, smell, and think. God is the only One who can see the whole picture. He sees beneath the surface. God knows who someone was in the past and who he or she will become in the future. How do we know that a person whom we see as a troublemaker or unfit will go through an entire life that way? Many peoples' lives are changed by God's touch. Saul was a perfect example. He was murdering Christians, and on the road to Damascus, the Lord changed his heart. His characteristics and name changed on that day. Paul went on to become devout Christian. It's only clear for God to see who will change and accomplish great works for Him (see, there's still hope for moms and dads!).

So how can this personality characteristic be turned into a positive characteristic for God? Search out employment, like law offices, where judgment is needed and encouraged. Judgment is discerning between right and wrong. Positive judgment is predominantly being the example, not the voice, of what we hold as God's truths.

If a profession is chosen where a judging nature is channeled into a positive forum, one can still follow in God's will. Teachers, policemen, executives can judge in a positive light and help and teach others to do the right things. Seats on a jury or on a board of education also utilize the gift of proper judgment. Stay-home parents can use judgment in a positive way. No matter which profession, healthy judgment is needed and utilized. Leave the judgment of someone else's future and soul to God.

Opinionated and outspoken people can play a big part in doing God's will as long as their judgments are used in the correct avenue. Being a member of a church board is a wonderful avenue for giving ideas about what should be done. Evangelists are usually opinionated and outspoken people who channel their opinions about the greatness of God to many people. Outspoken parents and grandparents can speak out about how proud they are and how much they admire their families for the Christian people that they are. Christian lawyers, social workers, activists stand up for what they believe in. There are many battered and torn children and adults who are not able to stand up for themselves. They need Christian advocates to be their voices.

The Busybody

Some red flags to watch for in identifying this overmeddling trait are as follows: Do you feel an excitement taking over your body while finding out all the details about what is going on in someone else's life? Do you have the desire to dig deeply and find facts about what may have led up to something else? Do you ever contemplate digging deep enough so that information gained can be used for leverage concerning something else?

Personally, I am guilty of crossing this sorry bridge many times. I even remind myself that it's none of my business. Truly, this is not the kind of person who I want to be. I should not get involved. The next thing I know, curiosity has taken over reasoning. I am knee-deep in casual gossip.

Some days it feels like being the chosen participant in reality TV. The problem lies in the fact that these moments are real life and not TV. The people who are involved are real people with real emotions. The biggest red flag should be that it's none of anyone's business! Everyone crosses this line from time to time.

Soul-searching in your deepest recesses should prompt some important questions. Why are you involved in this? Are you involved to truly offer help to this person or because of interest or curiosity?

Does the thought cross your mind that you may gain importance to others because of the information you attained? Are you using this time of discovery to avoid focusing on other necessary tasks? Are you involved because it leads to comparisons with your own life and relief that your life is in a less drastic state?

If the answer is yes to any other question other than genuinely offering assistance, rethink your involvement. If you are truly seeking God's plan for your life and asking Him, God will convict your hearts if changes are needed.

Put a positive spin on present lives by changing any negativity. So how is this accomplished with the "busybody" truth? Being a busybody can be a positive trait if it's executed properly. Churches and pastors benefit by being informed in healthy ways concerning emotional and physical states of church members.

Society today is very much geared toward social media. However, our aging congregation may not even be fluent with a computer, much less Facebook or Twitter. Many of our elderly residents, our homebound, are lonely and feel unimportant or forgotten. Sending them copies of the church bulletin or the monthly newsletter may not be sufficient.

A busybody could be a huge asset to a church by keeping in touch with people who are not able to attend or have moved. A special place in the bulletin could be reserved for "people scoop," telling bits and pieces of a beloved member's present life. It sends a message to members that out of sight does not mean out of mind.

A busybody could be helpful about connecting with busy pastors with desires or needs that might get overlooked. This helpful busybodying is not because pastors are not receptive or caring; they just can't often pick up on ten things at one time!

Righteous guidelines need to be set for healthy busybodies, both with God and with the church. The purpose of this interaction is nothing more than open communication. A very important and necessary stipulation needs to be set in stone for this policy to succeed. No information will be passed on to anyone, even pastors, without that member's consent.

This trust level has to be built in a congregation over time. The "busybodies" need to be considered trustworthy and take great pride in a sense of privacy.

Too Controlling

Believe it or not, the first warning for being too controlling comes from someone's own family. Granted, most children complain about parents controlling their lives, which is healthy and loving. For parents, many times the job of helping children to make well-thought-out decisions is not accepted as positively or appreciated as much by those who are being led. Remember feelings of parents stifling your life by not letting you have free reign? But looking back, you realize that your parents were helping you to stay safely out of potential trouble.

There is a difference between being a guiding person and a controlling person. Once again, the key to "improvements" is looking honestly within one's self. Listening to a doctor offering the remedy for an illness is a similar solution. If you really want to be in a healthier state, some serious questions have to be answered.

What is the purpose for inserting your authority in this situation? Are you seeking the well-being for this person? Are you seeking control of other people's ideas and all the steps along the way?

There are people on many church boards with innovative ideas that never make it to fruition because of a controlling board-head. These quiet "dreamers and planners" get silenced very quickly by people who like to hear only their own voices and ideas. A really effective committee head welcomes all ideas. After affirming and permitting an idea, the effective leader allows that person to run with the idea. There is no continual looking over one's shoulder and micromanaging.

Are you purposely showing off your own strength and authority? "I am the boss, and what I say goes!" Are you acting or reacting? Have you given any thought to the pros and cons of this decision? Is your final decision based on these pros and cons?

Are your controlling mannerisms based on how much you dislike change? Change is not an easy thing for anyone. Some people handle the uncertainty about trying a new thing better than others. Many times, people would rather have a familiar situation that is painful or no longer working than an unknown variable.

So here you are. You see yourself as *sometimes* controlling (I'll never admit to *always* being controlling). You truly love the Lord and want to be a vessel in His plan. So how does this personality trait of being controlling utilized in God's plan?

What are some jobs that call for the urges to control?

You might manage inventory control, keeping track of what is ordered and used. Being put in charge of something helps to alleviate that controlling tendency.

You may excel at planning a church outing by lining up details such as scheduling a bus, handling tickets, and making various stops along the way. A controlling person loves to be the deciding factor in times and outcomes.

Just a reminder to those who tend to be controlling: let others chime into big decisions such as the wheres and whens. An unhealthy situation occurs when a group of people feel like they are being manipulated and controlled. The best positive avenue for people who have a controlling urge is to control factors and not people.

Don't Play Well with Others

This imbalance causes stress every day in various environments during a typical day. Every week seems like high drama, whether at home, school, work, or church. There are always altercations, problems, and disagreements with other people. It seems like a shadow of negative air follows them around. Even gentle, easygoing people cringe at the thought of participating with these people in a group situation. Trouble follows them around, and they are high-maintenance.

Taking a hard look within in honesty and seeing this negative personality trait is hard to stomach. This negative characteristic of "not playing well with others" is the hardest characteristic to be brutally honest with yourself. The people who fall under this category would never naturally see or believe that they could ever be classified this way.

Take a look at some words that might be heard about a current mishap or altercation. (Now, granted, this might be the thirtieth altercation that they have lamented about in the last month. Do they see a pattern? No. Go figure!)

"It wasn't my fault." From their prospective, they were just doing what they were supposed to be doing.

All of a sudden, another person confronted them, tried to bully them, didn't include them, left them out of an important endeavor or tried to get them to do something that ethically they don't feel they should do.

The stages that follow are as follows: hurt feelings, bitterness, defensiveness, anger, threats to leave, or speaking to someone else about the issue. If presently experiencing a situation where the words about the "recent dilemma" are audible, probably that person is experiencing one of the stages after the hurt-feelings stage. They are probably belittling the person who "did them wrong" or emphasizing that they, of course, were blameless.

The peacemaker types try over and over to listen, to console, to understand, to give reconciling advice. After time passes, with numerous dilemmas, the peacemakers realize that they are giving advice to a deaf ear.

The "I don't play well with others" people do not see the connection between themselves and the problems that are happening. They cannot see how their actions initiate difficulties. They are not merely taking the blame off themselves; their tunnel vision blocks out the truth. They cannot see that they perpetrate the conflicts, even though everyone around them sees it!

"This is what I want." This expression of self-centeredness is familiar in conversations of another group of people who tends not to play well with others. "What's mine is mine, and what's yours is mine also" *is* a characteristic that starts appearing at birth.

The majority of human beings outgrow this two-year-old self-centeredness. As age progresses, we see situations by more of a global perception—the bigger picture.

People who don't play well with others only see what they want with tunnel vision. They have the same self-centered views as two-year-olds concerning what they want! Their indulgent desires at any given moment completely cloud their perspectives about other's needs.

"I am entitled." Self-centered natures are often coupled with entitlement. A certain treatment is deserved. Alice Boyes, PhD, describes some examples of red flags of entitlement and how to improve relationships after entitlement is identified.

Someone who feels entitled doesn't feel that rules applying to others do not necessarily apply to them. When working in groups, these people feel entitled to be the leader or to receive the most credit. A promotion or recognition should be given to them even though another is a more deserving candidate.

Red flags of conflict are the norm during interactions with people of entitlement. An "entitled" person is massively put out when a small request is asked of them yet consistently expects his or her desires to be a priority. Their goals, interests, and agendas are much more valid and necessary than others' lives. Social rules of common courtesy are often disregarded. If a meal is not served fashionably or correctly at a restaurant, a poor waiter or waitress publicly takes the brunt of the aggravation. Entitled people do not financially support frequently-used free gifts such as public television.

Relationships are strained often by inconveniences such as appointments canceled with no empathy for time spent in preparation by another. Perhaps a friend had to restructure his or her schedule to set it up in the first place. Store clerks can verify times when an entitled person came in to shop moments before closing, only to meander around at their own pace.

Fear of conflict is always in the air around people of entitlement. Those sharing space are usually walking on eggshells because offering upsetting or offending remarks are acceptable responses from entitled people. Peacemakers may be perceived as weak by choosing not to cause a conflict. When the scale is not in balance, relations tends to falter.

If these descriptions sound familiar and you want to improve the stability of relationships, it can be accomplished.

However, people with entitlement tendencies will react in two different ways. A select few do, in fact, realize their tendencies and feel motivated to change (I hope you are one of those few, if you struggle with this). The majority of entitled people see no reason to change and refuse. It's part of their DNA.

If you see these tendencies in yourself and want to gain more control of your actions, don't be too hard on yourself while working toward the end result. Expect consistent effort to change negative ways but be mindful of self-criticism. Harsh self-criticism results in a less positive change.

The first constructive change toward defeating the tendency of entitlement is to spend three minutes thinking about a recent altercation. During those moments, think only from the other person's perspective. Think about their agenda. Every time you feel an entitlement comment coming to mind about the situation, block it and go back to thinking of another's agenda.

Sensitize yourself to good emotions by mindfully promoting the success of another. Psychologists call this capitalization research, and it shows that by promoting others' successes, there will be a positive effect on the person promoting.

For one month, promote someone else's success every day.

Another way to improve entitlement tendencies is a psychological movement called cognitive restructuring. For every enablement tendency that you see, consider an alternate perspective. Question yourself. Why should some rules that apply to everyone else also apply to you? What are some reasons for keeping the peace and avoiding upsetting/offending people? Think of some examples of how people show you generosity more than you show to them.

Make note of reactions that happen when you curb your entitlement tendencies. Do relationships run smoother? Are you able to hold relationships longer because friends can relate to you in larger doses? Are you feeling more even—keel with less annoyances? Are people offering more support to you because you're supporting them a greater way? Curbing entitlement tendencies actually benefits you.

Catch yourself before you are led to the common tendency of justifying something that is wrong.

Being aware and honest with oneself about tendencies that interfere with relationships are the first steps to progressing to a more peaceful life. Entitlement tendencies create tunnel vision and keep you from the awareness of conditions those close to you may be going through.

"It's not fair." Entitlement means feeling deserving of things that are not deserved. But sometimes unfair decisions seem to prevail even with deserving time and effort put in.

Some friends don't play well with others and never seem to get a fair share at the things going on around them. Someone else got a promotion or a special job. Someone was awarded or complimented for his or her time, attitude, or effort. Another was awarded an important position in a team sport or a solo part in the band concert.

On the reverse side, the whole office was reprimanded for a negative performance rating. Disgruntled employees bristle because they bent over backward doing the correct things.

A new rule was created preventing fans from creating scenes at ball games. That's not fair. Everyone should be permitted to act in any way at their children's activities. Why should everyone be penalized for free speech?

Complaining aloud about things not being fair are trigger points to not getting along with others. If we hear these words coming out of our mouths, regardless of the circumstances, we need to stop in our tracks.

Mind the warning signs of your words. Make a conscious effort to tread cautiously on the roads ahead in how you react and the words that come out of your mouth. Satan may be laying his groundwork!

If you travel softly, the relationships in your life will improve. Homes, workplaces, friendships, and churches will improve with people working on being empathetic toward others.

CHAPTER 10

WORKING WITH GOD

"**I** have one nerve left, and you're stepping on it!" Does that sound familiar? We all experience the joy (and anguish) of being part of a group or service project and are presently at our wit's end.

In some ways, leaders are similar to jugglers. The leader has to be able to toss one ball and add more balls to combine with the first into a juggling act. All balls are recurring at the same time, and the juggler needs to be aware of each one.

A person in charge needs to be aware of each aspect of the project as part of the final finale. As a project moves forward, more and more elements are added. Like the juggler, to succeed, a leader must be aware of all the components.

When "in charge" of something, a primary decision must be made: do you desire help from others, or do you want to handle this project on your own? If you are willing to lead but tend to view the necessary volunteers as annoying participants who refuse to put the necessary time and effort into your high standards, a rocky road will be ahead. Often volunteers will complain that leaders will not present clear expectations upfront. These leaders will then find themselves huffing, bitter, and doing the tasks themselves to reach their high standards. Bitterness must be taken out for the duration of the project.

A leader's decision must be made at the starting point. A decision of handling a project alone leads to countless hours of preparation, orchestrating, and cleaning up done by a sole handler. This is a choice. If a leader chooses the help of others, clear expectations and directions must be allocated early on.

Preparation varies depending on the project. It could include researching, gathering details, setting agendas, copying, invitations, reserving location, and presenting. Preparation could also include decorating, organizing a menu plan, shopping, preparing, and baking. Preparation includes all the behind-the-scenes blood, sweat, and tears that most do not see.

Orchestrating a project requires some attributes that some people are blessed with, and some are not! Organization skills, time management, resource management are necessary to create a positive project. Obviously, depending on the project, a personal skill or background might be required. A noneducated person in a business field would not attempt a company presentation.

Cleaning up can contain lots of various tasks. Actually washing dirty dishes and utensils; dismantling stages, tables, and folding chairs; sweeping and mopping can be included in cleaning up. Cleaning up might include filing and note-taking. Everything that is taken out must be put away.

Lots of hard work for a person who wishes to ride solo!

A different decision is made for another project. The "leader" surveys all the balls in motion (like the juggler) and makes a list of all the needed components.

The next step is to D-E-L-E-G-A-T-E! Survey the people in close proximity. Who would be a good fit to take on this particular part of the project? Match that part of the project up with someone who flares in this area. (No one who is familiar with my talents would ever request for me to be in charge of decorations!)

If someone shoots down your request, don't get frustrated or give up. People need to feel the freedom to decline if a request isn't fitting for them at that time. No strings attached. That way, when a better opportunity opens up, that person will gladly jump in!

Once you have delegated a job, give some broad guidelines, if needed, and let go!

Be mindful of your own tendencies in leading. Desiring others' help but wanting things done solely within your guidelines creates a rigid workspace.

Sometimes, people in charge (including myself) have the whole picture set in their minds from start to finish. The whole stage is set in their minds: from decorations and types of materials needed, to agendas. The problem is that the "worker bees" don't have the same clear picture and idea, and it leads to frustration and anxiety on both ends. By taking a *hands-off* approach, the floor is open for creativity and pride for the volunteer who is offering assistance. A good leader is still juggling, setting up guidelines, and keeping an eye on the big picture without micromanaging.

Obtaining a successfully completed project often requires working hand in hand with others. The last chapter shed light on various personality types—other than yours, of course—and how they sound out in different scenarios. Characteristics like these may be experienced while working within a group. Remember, one nerve left and you're stepping on it? Be prepared to encounter interactions with others. Remind yourself that you cannot let Satan cause these quirks to run interference in reaching a final project destination.

While seeking to avoid dissention while in a *refueling* state, find something where attentiveness to detail and hard work can be done without interaction with others. There are many committees that need manual work done: cutting, mailing, sorting, one-on-one phone calls, compiling mailings, working on individual projects. Perhaps these services could be done in your own home during your desired time.

Being in-tune with your own inner working and faith level will promote decisions to create the space needed during a specific time frame to serve. God's workplaces should be positive and productive for everyone involved. It's most endearing to God when Christians take time to refuel their servant hearts. God knows that you are gaining the strength needed for the next job that He is calling you to do.

If working within a specific group makes your blood boil, make changes. We all have some qualities that, for some unknown reason, bother other people (*sigh*—I know, can you believe it?). But if the real goal is to improve our present walk with God, Christians have to be part of the solution.

Remember, Satan uses situations of high frustration and confusion to spin his evil web.

> For our struggle is not against flesh and blood,
> but against the rulers, against the authorities,
> against the powers of this dark world and against
> the spiritual forces of evil in the heavenly realms.
> (Ephesians 6:12, NIV)

Giving Satan less ammunition to hinder will empower you to take on the work that God has in store for you. When you feel like feelings of annoyance and anger are tying you up and bringing your servant's heart to a standstill, stop and rest.

Refuel with the power of God's Spirit through the Word. Wait for the flag beckoning you to start the race again, full speed ahead.

CHAPTER 11

DE-CLUTTER 101

Every day life is filled with feelings of anxiety and being on the edge. These are times when things are not handled the best way that they should. Every day life irritations or out-of-the-ordinary challenges bring out the worst. These occurrences happen often and sadly send one over the edge

Like many automobile accidents, many of these imminent quick-tempered moments could be avoided by knowing the source. If you determine trigger points that send you into this "unlovable" state, you could avoid a lot of hurtful times in relationships and life.

Some triggers frequently act as the starting point for this manic state.

Busyness is a prime example. Moments of the day are packed with so many things that there is a lack of time for yourself. Days are filled with to-do lists as soon as eyes open in the morning.

Automatically, brains are flooded with tasks: tasks from yesterday that are incomplete, tasks that need to be started today, tasks that you wish someday would be accomplished. (Do you have a room, corner, drawer somewhere that is your "throw-all" space? This junk drawer holds those little extra nails and screws that were placed in there over five years ago. Someday you are going to organize and clean out. Someday.)

Minimizing clutter and busyness is one of the first things needed to gain some control over your life (scary, isn't it?). Many times, busyness is used to cover over and mask thinking about any uncomfortable feelings. Allowing yourself to be constantly on the go prevents any open time to think about the state of your life!

The days have gotten busier and more hectic as years pass. Whether you are walking in the shoes of a stay-home mom or an office employee, worlds have gotten faster and more high-paced. Waiting for anything is not an option. Instant gratification is expected, and any delay is intolerable. Even eating and technology feed into this instant-gratification whirlwind.

Laundry centers have become the popular business around town. People can do multiple loads of laundry at one time so we are not tied to our houses during the few extra free moments that we have.

Most people don't take five minutes to reflect on a simpler life, much less the means to accomplish a simpler life. Every free moment is spent with to-do lists and errands that cause more feelings of being drained and irritable. The irritability is passed on to family or friends who are encountered as the minimal "personal" time is filled with unwanted errands. If something enjoyable like reading or relaxing is attempted, one is riddled with guilty feelings.

In my lifetime alone, I have witnessed many changes. Television used to have three channels, and at midnight, the screen would turn snowy. Stores were closed on Sundays. Time was spent in libraries to find needed information. Families had to talk face-to-face about plans because there were no cell phones. Computers were big, heavy furniture-style items that one might find in a huge business office.

Television channels, many restaurants, and grocery stores can be utilized twenty-four hours per day. Even small children have computers or cell phones that can be carried around with any information needed with one click. Cell phones can be used anywhere, even overseas. Photographs are taken more by cell phones than cameras.

"Declutter My Life 101" is a simple course to change the direction that lives are catapulting into. Make time every day to spend time with God. A specific time needs to be set aside in advance and not deviated from. Real "refrigerator" friends know what is essential to your happiness, and they will not try to dissuade you or distract you. Do not answer the phone, surround yourself with any distractions, or fit your special time in *after* all the other points on your to-do list. Give yourself permission to sit and talk to God.

> During this time, I commit my time to be surrounded by Your presence, Lord. Please open my ears, my eyes, my heart to focus this time on You.

If this commitment to meet with God is followed every day, life will not remain the same. God will minimize your clutter and give you clarification to your life.

For the first amount of time with God, listen to a worship or praise song, or talk to God about how much this small fraction of time in your day means to you. Let God know that you are now making Him a priority in your day. Many times, we perceive our special time with God with the attitude of a small child: "I want, I want, I want."

In a later chapter, we will talk about how to make this private time with God very effective. This is a time of thanking God for who He is and how thankful we are to have been born into His family. God does truly want to talk to us about what is on your heart, but these first couple of minutes are to give thanks to Him for who He is!

If we were told that God was truly coming to visit our home, we would drop everything to welcome Him into our homes, giving him our undivided attention.

God truly is visiting our homes. He delights in our willingness to be still and talk to Him. He delights in our quietness in listening to try to hear His voice! This quiet time with God is the first step needed in decluttering your life.

The second step is to ask God to open your ears and your heart to what He would like for you to hear. Then be quiet!

> He says, "Be still, and know that I am God; I will be exalted among the nations, I will be exalted in the earth." (Psalm 46:10, NIV)

The next step in "Decluttering 101" is looking at one surface of your day (imagine that!). Evaluate every part of your everyday life, from daybreak until falling into bed. How is this commitment being used to bring glory and honor to God's plan? What are the reasons for participating in this area? Am I acting as an *essential* vessel for God?

> For I know the plans I have for you," declares the
> Lord, "plans to prosper you and not to harm you,
> plans to give you hope and a future. (Jeremiah
> 29:11, NIV)

God has a plan in place for you. If you are filling your life with unnecessary noise, you will be unable to follow in His plan. The clutter and noise have to be reduced to truly listen to His calling.

There are many tugs on you through every waking hour. These strong pulls of busyness are put in your lives by Satan to distract you from doing the work that really matters. God does not want His gracious plan to feel overwhelming, impossible, or filled with negative, bitter thoughts. When truly playing a part in God's work, you feel energized, spiritually filled, and meaningful.

If you are not feeling that way, look closely at the whys. For what reasons are you doing this? Is God calling you to do this? When you are doing something truly for God's calling, you will feel spiritually energized.

An executive secretary whose high-pressure job gives her very little free time facilitates a project every year at Christmastime for poor families. This special project requires many facets, which have to be completed before this mission project is complete. Undertaking this whole process is exhausting to the person looking in from the outside.

This time-consuming project brings out more joy and energy than any other time of the year. My friend is truly giving herself completely to God's work, and it shows. God's light shines through her busyness, and her time is focused on Him! She comes alive because she is walking in His plan!

Are you involved in this commitment because a paycheck home is necessary?

A family in New York City spends on average $15,210 and $10,920 a year for child care for an infant and a school-aged child, respectively, according to a recent release from the office of Senator Kirsten Gillibrand (D-NY).

A job that pays $10 an hour amounts to an annual income of about $20,000, assuming the work is full-time. In 1970, more than 75 percent of single stay-at-home moms said they stayed at home to take care of their families. In 2012, only 41 percent of single stay-at-home moms said they're staying at home to take care of their families. The same share said they're staying at home because they can't find work, are ill, or have a disability. So in looking at the options, honestly, the time spent at this location is necessary.

Are you involved because you like socializing and knowing first-hand background facts about what's going on? Everyone likes to be in the front row for any breaking news, changes, excitement, or gossip. People also like to be in a ranking where they are enabled to have a voice in the way things are handled or completed. Churches have committees filled with grumbling, voicing opinions, complaining, but not joyfully engaging in active, joyful Christian service. Look at your underlying purpose for your opinions. Is your purpose to create a wonderful environment for worship?

Do you feel obligated to participate? I made a terrible motherly mistake when my daughter was a teenager. I was so happy that she was actively involved in church that I strongly encouraged her to volunteer as much as possible. I did not see the fact that she was trying so hard to please her mom that she became bitter about the volunteering busyness.

If you are serving God more frequently by obligation and not by a joyous heart, this is an act of busyness and not worship. This service is clutter and should be removed.

Be honest with yourself. Ask, am I truly doing this commitment as work given to God or for other reasons? Am I acting as an *essential* vessel for God's work?

One recent problem that many churches face is the same people serving over and over on committees. These faithful people are burned out, worn very thin, and have very little energy to input into doing God's projects. If these faithful people are asked (and these are faithful people because they love God and our churches), many predictable responses would be that no one else would volunteer and someone had to do it.

As individuals, you need to ask yourself if you are acting as an essential vessel. God wants great things to happen to churches. Love and energy need to be put into areas that God is working. Faithful people get spread so thin that their works are forced to be mediocre.

People should be encouraged to declutter their service by giving up useless time and energy. That energy needs to be focused on specific areas that God is calling them to do. By breathing this breath of air and excitement, giving and doing for God, other quieter members will feel exhilarated.

So if you are one of those tired, spread-too-thin faithful servants, seek God's will for your life. You'll know which area it is. Like my friend, you will feel an excitement and energy that drives you. Don't feel like you have to do service that drains your energy on a long-term basis. It's different to volunteer occasionally to help with an activity that is not in your comfort zone to help out the bigger picture.

Friends who know me personally know that I am much more of a Mary than a Martha. Organizing church dinners, planning our soup-kitchen menu, celebratory lunches are all areas far out of my comfort zone. However, I am always willing to help out occasionally by chopping carrots, peeling potatoes, or breaking apart lettuce for a salad. Just give me exact directions, and I will gladly help with a task. It's okay to clearly admit that this is out of your comfort zone to be in charge or to organize such an event.

God gives all needed strength and wisdom needed to learn how to utilize the gifts that are given—one surface at a time.

What are some of the surfaces that demand your attention? Children? Spouse? Church? Job? Friends? Pets? Commitments? Yoga? Gym? Exercise classes? Book clubs? Weight-management classes? These are all good commitments and activities to be involved in.

When are those times when you feel most peaceful and can step out of the craziness? Think of a time when you are not consumed with a to-do list or feeling guilt. Reading a good book? Going to the gym? Playing with your dogs? Taking a friend for a coffee or lunch?

Each is wired differently. Before being able to improve your days and giving yourself this gift of time, answer some questions about yourself.

Do you get a burst of energy, or are you drained of energy from being around other people? If something bad happens at work, would you prefer to drink a cup of coffee by yourself and regroup, or call friends and tell them all the details of your challenging day? When do you feel more intact and ready to face a problem, after you do something physical, meditate, or something spiritually related or something quiet like sewing or needlepoint?

Shortly after getting married, I signed up for a sewing class. After all, a good wife mends her husband's pants, right? Some amusing self-history: when I had the choice in middle school to participate in home economics or shop, guess what I picked? I built a wonderful candleholder out of wood! Everyone said that sewing was so relaxing and helped so much with stress and yada, yada, yada. Well, let me just tell you—after sewing class, I was more stressed out than writing a ten-page term paper!

So know yourself. Personally, I do like quiet alone time when I am facing problems, or I'm having a bad day. I prefer sitting on my front porch with a cup of coffee and my dogs—not sewing!

Give yourself permission to do something whimsical instead of feeling guilty for time not spent on other tasks. Make a date with yourself: during this fifteen minutes, I am not going to hurriedly do other tasks. Think whimsical!

Unfortunately, other areas often take precedence over doing something positive for yourself. Fun and freeing moments during the week should be frequent! Just be sure that there is a difference between fun and freeing moments and the busyness that controls your life.

How to manage time is a valuable asset to hold. Time management is the only key for making sure that the important people in your life always feel important. Those important people to you shouldn't feel squeezed in. Convey to others the unbending reality.

Those people are very important, and there is no wavering here, no gray areas.

Now, that's not to say, telling an employer that you are leaving your job early to take my child to the movies. But if it's an emergency and my child is sick, you will be there. Scheduled times are helpful in creating valuable time choices. If you schedule a specific time on a schedule, in a short time, those around you will recognize your routine and try not to schedule things during your allotted appointment. By prioritizing your life and the important things, some of the unnecessary busyness and clutter will be reduced.

Do an inventory of meaningful, important things in your life. Now sequence them according to need and importance. Financial? Needed. School activities? Important. Shopping? Depends. What are the areas that you wished you had more time allotted to focus on? Are there areas that are taking your time that you wish you could reduce to spend more time on other areas? What are the items on your to-do list?

CHAPTER 12

FIGHTING NEGATIVE FEELINGS

The battle starts as soon as feet hit the floor in the morning. You have managed to cut a lot of previous anxieties by simplifying and prioritizing events, but a lot of modifications remain to be done. Sometimes negative feelings start flooding in. You fight feelings of not being special, no longer needed, ill-equipped, overwhelmed, which are hurtful, negative feelings. These are the kinds of feelings that will paralyze you and hinder you from doing meaningful things for God.

Satan uses negative feelings like this to cause division in families and cause you to feel incompetent and insecure.

Insecurity at home happens with change, criticism, and negativity. Perhaps a loved one gets involved in other interests. The atmosphere of the home changes. Your perception of the once-beloved relationship seems distant and forced. This happens especially with children when they reach the teenage years. Sports, friends, significant others, outside activities fill their calendars. Parents are left in the dust, wondering how that affectionate person, who loved tinkering with cars and family meals, disappeared. You are left with a feeling of unimportance and lack of appreciation.

Insecurity in workplace is another festering source of negative feelings. Workplaces are filled with young minds and the latest technology. Perhaps this resounds with you. You have always felt competent and knowledgeable, but lately, the feelings feel more like you are a gerbil on a wheel getting nowhere. People bustle around me and speak of latest changes in the infrastructure that I know nothing about. Is my contribution needed anymore? Will I be needed here much longer?

Resentment is another feeling that grows into a black mountain. Why do things come so easily for this person? Why do I take so much time to do things the right way, and this person gets away with skimming the surface? Why does money seem to fall into other laps, and I am left always robbing Peter to pay Paul?

Fear of failure is another sure way to increase the number on the negative-feeling dial. Ugh. Why try this when every time it results in failure? You feel disheartened that no one will ask you to do anything because of your track record of failures in the past. You feel as though you should give up before you even start.

If God asked you personally, face-to-face, to do something, you would jump right in with no fear of failing. You wouldn't even look back. The problem lies in the questioning of whether God is truly leading. You fear that perhaps it is your own mixed-up mind leading you into disaster, mistakenly thinking that it is God nudging.

Sometimes those negative voices imply that it's not God whom you are hearing. Why would God desire for you to even try and make a mess?

Minds act as extremely top-notch editors with the highest standards. Every past mishap or slightly nonpar attempt is filed perfectly, and file recovery is split second and on the mark. However, you drastically fall short in the "satisfactory" category for the majority of successes from your past. Somehow the details of the past positive attempts get lumped into one filing of "good days." The details get muddled, and nothing really stands out as top-of-the-line.

How can this filing imbalance be remedied? After completing an activity of service, allot ten minutes to think about only positive aspects. It's human nature: after orchestrating an activity, you watch your mind play back the events. So the sequence is for you to decide. Think through your usual negative and positive playback first or second. As you replay the event in your mind, if the scene is negative, stop. Think of corrections that could improve it.

If you choose to think through the complete playback first, make sure to designate ten minutes to thinking solely of strong, positive parts. This is your "note to self" filed away for future use. The newly modified items can be inserted into this file as well.

Think of corrections that would lead to improvement. Set your thought process apart from biting, critical comments. Step away from your natural response of anger and defense over these comments. If the remedy is easily satisfied, apply it, whether you agree with it or not. People have a harsh way of presenting their requests, even if their requests are doable. On the flip side, if you are the one handing out constructive criticism, your presentation plays a huge role in how your opinions are received!

This is the file that can be pulled up when those uneasy or negative pangs are felt.

Body image is another issue that creates a truck bed full of negative feelings. Do you ever catch yourself cringing when you see your reflection in a mirror? Given a choice between a room with a large mirror, or a room with no mirror to pass, would you choose the room with no mirror?

Steven Curtis Chapman wrote a song "Only One and Only You" for his wife that really sums it up. Like his wife, do you ever find yourself looking in a window at the reflection or scarier yet, in a mirror, and are unimpressed by the reflection looking back? Look at all of the wear and tear! What happened? Does the mirror seem to point out decades of pounds have made themselves comfortably at home in your body? Does your big athletic accomplishment of the day entail going up and down 2 flights of steps doing laundry?

I used to be an athlete in high school one hundred years ago, so I was in good physical shape (bikinis? Scary memory). I was 117 pounds when I got married and pregnant with my first child. Now I look in the mirror, and decades of pounds have made themselves comfortably at home in my nonathletic body. My big athletic accomplishment for the day is going up and down two flights of steps with laundry!

In the old days, I used to daydream about John Travolta using me as his disco dance partner. Now I listen over and over to Steven Curtis Chapman's love song to his wife, daydreaming that my husband thinks I'm "better than a Beethoven symphony and that Mona

Lisa wishes that she could be as beautiful as you." Thanks, Steven Curtis Chapman, for being my midlife hero!

The culture blushes and puts beautiful thin or handsome petite humans on pedestals. In the last several years, large clothing distributors and designers have created more commercials and models to stand apart in the plus-size category. However, the culture still places a lot of weight (catchword, eh?) on a person's figure and style.

Wouldn't you love to read results of a hypothetical survey counting the number of people at routine physical at doctor's office, grimacing when they are given the "obese" description after the weigh-in. Just saying.

This is the time needed for self-evaluations and honesty. If you wish to build a better life, you need to be brutally honest with yourself. No more outward appearances used to help sway others. Truth!

Why are you thinking about your appearance? Are you trying to appear differently than you truly are? Do you worry about judgment from what you look like? Sure, losing some pounds would be ideal. Sure, some defined muscles would look good. There are fine lines between striving for a goal, obsessing, and portraying a false picture underneath.

> So God created mankind in His own image, in
> the image of God He created them; male and
> female He created them. (Genesis 1:27)

God created you with a multitude of good qualities in His own image. You are reading this book, so hopefully, your goal is to try to get rid of negative feelings and build a better life. In order to succeed at that goal, never second-guess God in how He created you. Yes, most have sabotaged many attributes that were His blessings by poor choices.

So the first step in getting rid of negative feelings concerning appearance is honesty about the person who you are within. You can strive to bring that person out in positive ways. The confidence will start shining through when you stop trying to mask who God intended you to be. Be mindful of how negative thoughts are impacting your present life. Many times, you won't even realize how much damage is being done. Start focusing on powerful, positive thoughts.

God created you a certain way for a reason. Once you truly accept the person you see in a mirror and resolve feelings of dissatisfaction, you will put that nagging dislike of your appearance to rest. Your life will improve, one surface at a time.

CHAPTER 13

How to Get Along Better

Whether you are a parent, child, or an employee, being competent is an essential attribute. The worst attack would be to be outwardly proven to be unfit and incompetent. Satan weaves a very tangled web to make this misconception happen.

God has a plan for your life. He works through you as His vessels. If Satan came and directly telling you not to be God's vessel, certainly you would not allow it to happen. But Satan places roadblocks between you and whom you'll interact with in service to God. Satan wants you to question your own competence, integrity, and abilities. If you allow yourself to feel threatened, the questions and insecurities will mount, causing a blockage between others and yourself. Satan causes friction through another person. Maybe another person questions, disagrees, or goes behind your back.

The initial feelings are anger and resentment. How can someone do this? The anger escalates to a judgment step, where mental comparisons are made to them. This is the step where you probably defend yourself and angrily question the right for another to have an opinion at all.

Hurt feelings are the next secession. However, anger and resentment often mask these feelings. Only painful honesty will bring acknowledgement of the hurt to the surface, allowing the resolving process to begin. Bringing hurt feelings to the surface can be very time-consuming. Hurt feelings are often viewed as weaknesses; unlike strengths associated with anger. It's much easier to remain in the anger and resentment stage rather than admitting a vulnerability. However, the longer the anger and resentment stage lasts, the more time passes before conflict resolution begins.

The natural instinct as human being, is to protect oneself. Because of needed protection, the hurt feelings quickly turn into bitterness. For the duration of this conflict, that's where these feelings remain. Through the entire conflict, focus will continue to be on the other person's attack.

Are you ever able to personally separate yourself from this situation by realizing that Satan is working here? These attacks and bitterness are filed away in your heart. Satan keeps track of these incidents and uses them to build his tower of deception. He will work through another person, another incident, and another challenge. Once in a while, he will bring this incident to the surface again just to remind you that it happened. You could be reminded of these feelings through many avenues: songs, smells, memories, words on a card or page, and pictures. Satan will use these memories to build his house of deception, questioning your confidence in yourself over time.

Ask God to shine His light on the picture. From a person's view, Satan's tower looks like a very strong, secure, never-to-be-moved, overwhelmingly tall tower. But God's light shone on the surface shows that this tower is made from deception. Like cards, these blocks are really paper-thin.

God wants you to see the real picture. If Satan is using people in your world to frustrate, anger, or scare you, remind yourself that your faith in God is built upon a rock. The battle has already been won. The ending to the story is already revealed. Please see through God's light and don't give Satan the chance to build his weak tower to question your confidence.

God created you to be compassionate, sensitive, emotional people. You were created in His image. The problem surfaces because sinful nature hinders you from discerning negative feelings that you have. Often, simple emotions convert into a roller coaster. Soon feelings are not connected to the original emotion at all. An avalanche of out-of-control negative feelings paralyze and control.

One technique in getting along better is named the 60 percent/40 percent system. Fifty percent /50 percent? Isn't that what all perfect marriages and friendships are supposed to be—50 percent/50 percent? That is one of those ideals that live happily in our minds, but it just doesn't exist in reality. People in a relationship, whether it is in a marriage or friendship, function on different levels of the 50 percent ladder. A person is having an easier, stronger day and the other a weaker or more stressful day.

To work as a healthy team member, be willing to lead or be willing to follow, depending on whether you find yourself in the 60 percent or the 40 percent on that given day. That means, if you are the 60 percent, you will need to pull a little bit more weight than usual for your partner. Emptying the dishwasher, driving children to activities, mowing the grass, or getting emissions testing done on a car might creep onto your to-do list. Whatever the task, on this day, my partner is the 40 percent, and I am the 60 percent.

Fly through life in formations like geese. Len Wilson, Christ follower and writer, says it perfectly! The following is excerpted and reformatted from a manuscript I am editing titled "Lead Like Butler: Six Principles for Values-Based Leaders" by Kent Millard and Judith Cebula (Abingdon 2012).

> Every fall thousands of geese fly from Canada to the southern part of the United States to escape the bitterly cold Canadian winter. As soon as a flock of geese take flight from Canadian waters they quickly form a V-shape flying pattern, with one rotating goose in the center lead and all the other geese trailing behind in two close lines.
>
> Wildlife scientists have conducted extensive studies to determine why geese and other migratory birds always fly in a distinctive v-formation. They found some fascinating results:
>
> When geese fly together, each goose provides additional lift and reduces air resistance for the goose flying behind it. Consequently, by flying

together in a v-formation, scientists estimate that the whole flock can fly about 70% farther with the same amount of energy than if each goose flew alone. Geese have discovered that they can reach their destination more quickly and with less energy expended when they fly together in formation. When people work together harmoniously on teams, sharing common values and a common destination, they all arrive at the destination quicker and easier, because they are lifted up by the energy and enthusiasm of one another.

When a goose drops out of the v-formation it quickly discovers that it requires a great deal more effort and energy to fly. Consequently, that goose will quickly return to the formation to take advantage of the lifting power that comes from flying together. Sometimes people playing on teams will drop out of the group and try to accomplish goals on their own. However, like the geese, they usually discover that they miss the synergy and energy that comes when they are an active part of a cohesive team moving toward their destination, and want to return to the group.

Geese rotate leadership. When the goose flying in the front of the formation has to expend the most energy because it is the first to break up the flow of air that provides the additional lift for all of the geese that follow behind the leader. Consequently, when the lead goose gets tired, it drops out of the front position and moves to the rear of the formation, where the resistance is lightest, and another goose moves to the leadership position. This rotation of position happens many times in the course of the long journey to warmer climates. When a team is functioning well, various members of the team may take the leadership role for a while because of a particular expertise or experience. Consequently, on good teams, everyone has the opportunity to serve as a leader as well as a follower.

Geese honk at each other. They also frequently make loud honking sounds as they fly together. Scientists speculate that this honking is their way of communicating with each other during their long flight. Similarly, when working on teams, it is exceedingly important for each team member to communicate regularly with all the other team members. Teams frequently fall apart because of the lack of adequate communication among the various members of the team. Perhaps human teams can learn from flying flocks of geese that constant communication among members is exceedingly important in moving effectively towards a common destination.

Geese help each other. Scientists also discovered that when one goose becomes ill, is shot or injured, and drops out of the formation, two other geese will fall out of formation and remain with the weakened goose. They will stay with and protect the injured goose from predators until it is able to fly again or dies. Likewise, human teams work best when they do more than just work together, but care for the well being of each other.

Isn't it interesting how God gives the helpful needed advice for living the 60/40 percent system right in front of our own eyes? It is almost a guarantee that each person who is reading this book can honestly say they have watched the geese formation flying overhead at least five times. How to improve our relationships can be learned from geese.

The leader gets tired, admits that he is tired, and welcomes the substitute leader while taking his part of the rotation in the back. Sometimes Christians strive for their own independence and identity. They briefly try to function on their own but soon learn that it's much harder to fly without teammates to help.

You can fly much further distance with others in the formation than you can try on your own using the same amount of strength. Communication keeps the team from falling apart before arriving at the common destination. If a member gets down or hurt, it's your job to stay with that person and protect them while they're down. It's comforting and powerful for all to have security that someone has your back!

So lead when you are strong, follow when you are weaker, and realize that both roles are very important in the relationships of your life. Knowing this will make every step of the journey a little easier.

CHAPTER 14

GO GREEN

Improving how people interact and react to one another will create a healthy environment around you. Environments become more peaceful for those who enter the shared space a lot. Whether it is with families, or workplaces, or churches, a conscious effort can be made to improve personal space in the present.

Too often, prayers are lifted for God to improve a certain situation or environment, but the person offering the prayer is unwilling to play a part in improving it. (yes, sometimes I, myself, *am* part of the dynamics!) The environment is seen as a stressful place with obligation to be a part of. Your present can't be improved unless you take ownership of your roles and actions.

In a busy world, moments that could help with improvements are probably overlooked. Actively take notice of the people around you and then verbally acknowledge them. Every person has the desire to be cherished and appreciated. If it's a family member who has been working very hard on a school assignment, you could say, "Wow, I can see all the time you put into that. I hope you get a grade that reflects the work you put into it!"

If it's an employee at work, make notice of some positive attribute. "I wish I was as organized as you are" or "The snacks you brought in to our employee lounge are just what I needed, to get through the rest of the day."

Pay attention to a person's demeanor.

"You really seem like you're carrying a heavy weight. Is everything okay? "Sometimes, that opens the door for further discussion.

89

"I don't know why the coach picked someone else to play that position," or

"My teenager is having boy problems and I was awake almost all night," or

"I just got a new pile of papers on my desk, and I feel swamped."

They probably don't need or desire help to "fix" the problem. Others appreciate affirmation that you notice what state they're in. You might respond with the fact that you are so sorry, asking if there is anything you can do to help- the verbal hug, just to let them know you care.

When you find yourself in the middle of a conflict, look through the other person's eyes and see a different perspective. Everyone is guilty at times for looking at situations, through only one perspective. That tunnel -vision keeps from focusing on the whole picture.

Do you ever hear imaginary voices speaking in your mind? Those voices assure you that of course you are correct and you don't deserve to be treated this way. The voice may remind you that this is not a huge problem. People won't even remember tomorrow. There is no other way but your way to accomplish this end.

Having one's feelings validated and acknowledged is important to most Christians. For whatever reason, emotions are definitely present and minimizing them is not an option of choice. By trying a new approach, your voice may still be heard and others are not put on the defensive.

Acknowledge that you view this challenge differently. Offer to share your ideas if others are willing to hear a new prospective or to gain more dimensions.

Sometimes, a person is not accepting feedback because of the mood that they are in. If that's the case, respond that you see that, at this moment, they are angry and lashing out, without seeing the picture in whole. Remind them that you are willing to speak when things settle down.

Humans are also egocentric. The only things that naturally pop up on radars are issues that exist in their own lives. Remind yourself, often, not to always talk about your life, your concerns, your hardships, your great moments, and your strengths.

Give yourself a challenge today. Make a conscious effort to not speak of yourself for a whole day. Catch yourself every time you start to mention yourself or your life. Turn your focus onto asking that person something about themselves and their lives.

Often, when challenges or hardships are taking place, people don't want others to *fix* the problem. They just desire validation of the struggle and support. Inquire if they're doing okay and pass on your empathy that they are going through this. Portray to them that you can see and feel how hurt they are. Ask them to let you know if you can do anything to help. Chances are that there is nothing you can do. However, acknowledging and validating their feelings opens the channel of support.

By taking an active part, in making your present environments more positive and healthy, the majority of your days will be markedly improved. Soon, the positive attitudes will become more of a natural habit and you won't have to remind yourself to look beyond your own issues.

> But someone will say, "You have faith; I have deeds. Show me your faith without deeds, and I will show you my faith by my deeds. (James 2:18-NIV)

> No matter in which environment you spend the majority of your days, your faith is shown by your actions. By cherishing those people around you, even those we really don't like, you are wearing our faith in Jesus Christ.

In the 1960's, Peter Scholtes wrote the perfect song verbalizing this concept.

"They Will Know We Are Christians by Our Love"

We will work with each other; we will work side by side
We will work with each other; we will work side by side
And we'll guard each man's dignity and save each man's pride
And they'll know we are Christians by our love, by our love
Yeah, they'll know we are Christians by our love."

The people who are constant in our lives need to know that nothing they can do or say will keep us from loving them. I may not always *like* you, but I am in this relationship for the long haul. Unconditional love is a valued key in improving our relationships. This treasury of love is only possible if the bad and the ugly are accepted along with the good. It's a package deal. Don't try to mold someone into someone they are not.

In 1966, there was a Walt Disney movie called "The Ugly Dachshund" about a Great Dane who believed he was a dachshund. The husband in the movie (Dean Jones) wanted a Great Dane. His wife (Suzanne Pleshette) owned small dachshunds and competed in prize dog shows. One day, Dean Jones brings home a male puppy and tells his wife he is a dachshund puppy. Well, the rest of the movie is one belly laugh after another.

The point is crystal clear, as much as Dean Jones tries to make his Great Dane into a beloved dachshund, it's impossibility. A Great Dane will be always a Great Dane.

Some of the characteristics of people in your life can be modified, but the meat underneath is still the same as the day of their births. You can't change the DNA of people in your life. However, you can accept them as a package deal, bad with the good.

"You get what you get and you don't get upset" is the old expression that speaks the truth. Thankfully, God created everyone differently (thank goodness many idiosyncrasies are not hereditary!)

One direction of thinking needed to improve present life is the realization and acceptance of differences. After this most difficult stage, these strengths need to be utilized in your every day world.

As Christians, the mission in this lifetime is to bring others to get to see the incredible treasure map that Christians are privy to. Often these telling opportunities are missed because differences in people block the way.

Knocking down the walls of tunnel vision will allow you to tidy up your life. Appreciate and utilize the many strengths and differences that are right in front of your face. Thank God, the Artisan, for all of the masterpieces that He has created. You may even learn something about your own self along the way. Scary right?

Look for positive traits instead of constant criticism whether someone is within your inner circle or not. Perhaps your spouse always watches too much T.V. and never gets the yard work done. Think of this in a different perspective. Sure, you wish that you got more yard work done, but you are so blessed to have a spouse that enjoys being at home instead of running around.

How do you react to someone who is being unkind or abrupt? Before you react, remind yourself that only half of the picture can be seen. The trigger for someone's reaction is not clearly seen. Did some event recently cause this person to be in a bad mood? Perhaps being too overly sensitive at that moment projects a false picture. This picture leads to over-reaction on your part.

Personally, I find myself feeling on guard when my husband comes home from work. Often, I feel he is distant, and not super excited to see me. In reality, he has had a long, irritating, hour and a half drive home from work. He needs a few moments to unwind.

Necessity to work in different time- frames can cause unnecessary friction between people as well. Faithful people are willing to put energy into completing a project. They maneuver all the pieces to the puzzle, rearranging parts, until completion. The end product is exemplary.

However, friction occurs when they feel forced to work under time frames different from their own. Extended time is needed by some in organizing a project to completion. Surely, you can identify people, who cautiously and tenderly organize and rearrange working parts, to fit their standards.

Others, however, seem capable of accomplishing a great deal within very little time. Thriving when time restrictions are near, they rise to success with last minute changes.

If your spouse or co-worker is someone who needs time to sort things out, don't throw a big idea in his or her corner at the last minute. That will surely throw that person into a tizzy. If your child, spouse or co-worker thrives in last minute completion, take the reigns off. Let them work in that hurried pace, without nagging them to see that the project gets finished.

The key to successfully accepting others' time management is the successful completion of the project. If projects are drawn out, or overlooked, negative emotions come into play and the nagging begins. Avoiding negative interactions promotes healthy environments and successful projects, in homes or work places.

You've subtracted negative clouds in your environment, and now the time has come to add positive layers as well. Building better relationships by knowing personalities of others creates healthier and more productive environments.

Gary Chapman wrote several books about the five languages of love, which can change your whole perspective on relationships with others. These writings are an immensely valuable tool to learn concrete ways to improve present relationships, regardless of the age or relationship connection that you are trying to improve.

Humans show love or kindness in five ways: physical contact, words of affirmation, acts of service, gifts, or spending time.

The five love-languages decipher how someone is showing and receiving love. It could be a child, parent, friend, and co–worker. If you want to improve or strengthen a relationship, whether it is a close relationship or a work atmosphere, learn how to show love. It's similar to trying to fluently speak an important message in a foreign language you are unfamiliar with. Of course, the foreigners smile but they really don't understand your words. Putting forth the effort time and time again, you attempt to tell them your message. Frustration and confusion gradually heap up on both sides. Then, all of a sudden, someone comes along and translates your message and the important message is understood, loud and clear. Gary Chapman is that translator!

Your predominant love-language is not the only way that you will extend feelings of love to another. The range of emotions and love-connections is very profound. Greeks identify different kinds of love. Mateo Sol helpfully describes these different types of love.

Eros or erotic love is sexual passion and desire named after the Greek god of love and fertility. *Philia* is affectionate, friendship love between equals. Plato felt that physical attraction was not a necessary component of love. (That's where the word platonic originated.)

Philia is the kind of love felt between two friends who have gone through a lot of happy and challenging times together. *Storge* or familiar love primarily involves kinship, (e.g. parents and children, or childhood friends who are "adopted family.)

Ludus is the playful love you may see in early stages of falling in love like flirting, teasing, heart palpitating.

Pragma is enduring love that has aged, developed and matured over time. This type of love is found in couples that have been together for many years or friendships that have survived for decades. Unfortunately, this type of love is unique and hard to find because so much time and energy is spent trying to find love, and so little time spent in learning how to maintain it. Hopefully, after reading *One Surface at a Time*, perhaps steps can be taken to turn most love into *pragma* love!

Philia is deep friendship and loyalty. Soldiers fighting side by side may feel this faithful friendship and sacrificing.

Philautia is self- love. Greeks felt that the only way one could love others; one must learn to care for oneself. This type of love is not an unhealthy type of self–obsession or vanity that is focused on personal fame, gain and fortune like narcissism. This love is the strength to feel comfortable in your own skin. Aristotle said that all friendly feelings for others are an extension of a man's feelings for himself.

Agape love is selfless, unconditional, spiritual love. This type of love is infinity of empathy and compassion. Agape is a pure form of love, free from desires, expectations, flaws or shortcomings.

Within every form of love, Gary Chapman's wisdom of the five languages of love can be utilized. By orchestrating love and caring for others in your life, warmth and peace will occur. Relationships will improve. Much less time will be spent on negative energy and differences. Aggravation and misconception will occur less frequently.

Count all the relationships in your life, even salty relationships. By learning to identify and speak a person's foreign language, whether you care for them or not, your connection with that person is sure to improve. Your present environment will be changed in a very positive way, one surface at a time.

CHAPTER 15

CONSTRUCTION ZONE

I f you are moving toward that place of self-honesty, you are coming to the realization that there are areas in your life that you know are wrong. You know in your heart that you are not supposed to go that route, and yet before realizing it, you're heading down that path.

My city has been doing major pipework on a road for about six months. Driving on this road is bumpy, uneven, irritating, and extremely time-consuming. Sometimes the road is passable, yet other times, a portion of the road is closed, and cars have to detour down side roads. I know about the construction on this road and have experienced the problems multiple times. Yet I find myself driving on this awful road even after I make a mental note while leaving my house that I am going to drive an alternate route.

There are areas in life that are the same. Detours, bumps, uneven and irritating bends come. Sometimes you land on these challenges by accident. You have no control over these surprises. Numerous times, however, you know that patch is ahead. Deep within, you know that you don't want to go there. Yet, by habit, you find yourself doing the same regrettable things over and over again.

Assortments of bad habits are struggled with every day. Concern about bad habits is generally pushed under a carpet of excuses. Are any of these excuses familiar to you? Not being able to teach an old dog new tricks, that's just who you are, there are many habits worse than the kind that you are confronted with, so why waste your precious time obsessing about it? You just went along with it because people from work wanted to. (How old are we? Still dealing with peer pressure?)

If you know that a certain person or group leads you into an area that might cause bumps or challenges, change the routine. If friends from work are going out after work, and when you participate, you arrive home late, miss family events like sports games, fight a pull of alcohol addiction—change the protocol. Be upfront and stand strong. Tell your fellow employees that you are sorry but must decline because your family is your priority.

Try to detour situations where you are more apt to hit the bumps of regret.

When you must encounter a construction zone unexpectedly and a detour is not available, take the high road. Don't let yourself get coaxed into anger, frustration, or even road rage. Plans often change, and flexibility can avert many disasters.

Many valuable lessons are learned while teaching a teenager to drive (not only the important lesson that your life is precious!).

Always learn from your mistakes and don't ever give up. Mistakes are made every day, from getting out of bed until tucking the covers in at night. You have the choice of following through with the negative feelings that come with the mistakes or trying again. Those negative voices remind you that you can't do this, you're not very good at this, and someone else could perform this job better than yourself. "I'm going to do this same thing wrong over and over again, so why try?" These negative thoughts shoot you down before you even get started! Ask God to give you strength when you hit the bumps, and He will offer His help during our downfalls.

Christians sin every day. Satan quietly whispers that you will not succeed. Why not let someone who is more talented and efficient take the helm? Why shouldn't that person do more anyway? You attempted this before, and all that came off it was stress and misery, so why would you want to put yourself in that position again?"

As a parent, sitting next to this frequently-frustrated driver, you see a bigger picture than she can see. You can see past the frustrations to a very wonderful feeling of independence and opportunity. God sees a much bigger picture than you can see. Like a parent, He knows of the challenges and struggles that you are facing right now. You feel like throwing in the towel because things are not easy. Of course, He is a better driver than you, but His desire is for you to gain confidence and venture out on your own. He promises that He is right by your side. You can ask Him anything, talk with Him about any fears or insecurities. He is here! Don't quit—good things lie ahead for those who wait and stick in there.

> My Father's house has many rooms; if that were not so, would I have told you that I am going there to prepare a place for you? (John 14:2, NIV)

Look ahead and plan. Young drivers are taught to make a plan of action ahead of time for the challenges that may come up. When the light changes, which lane are you going to be in? What do you think the other cars are going to do? Be smart. Sometimes other drivers don't follow the rules, so you have to drive defensively and watch their moves. Know ahead of time how to face challenges that may come.

The same truth helps you in your present life today. Look ahead and know your plan before the challenge comes. If you can avoid this challenging intersection ahead, go a different way. If it cannot be avoided, have a plan in place before you are caught in the oncoming situation.

There will be situations where someone regularly disobeys the rules. If you are looking ahead and might find yourself in the center of this problem by going this way, make an alternate plan. Detour around any unnecessary challenges or temptations whenever possible.

Be aware of what's going on around you. Flat tires, mail trucks pulling out, road construction, cars pulled over by police—are obstacles that come up every day. Be aware and do not travel with tunnel vision so that you can protect others and ourselves

Check your indicators. Don't run out of gas before arriving at your destination. Many times, Christians eagerly volunteer to serve on committees. The enthusiasm is true and real. But before even realizing it, the fuel has diminished, and your body comes to an abrupt halt. The indicators have been warning you: overly tired, frustrated, and stressed beyond words. Yet you continued onward in this haggard path, thinking that a good Christian doesn't get tired or make excuses. Now the choice cannot be made on your own. The body is telling you that your intentions are good, but it is out of gas. You've come to a dead halt, wishing that you had elected for some refilling times of mind, body, and spirit. It's really important to keep in God's Word and not just get caught up in the busyness of servanthood.

> Yet I hold this against you: You have forsaken the
> love you had at first. (Revelation 2:4, NIV)

Whether nearby or far away, everything that a Christian should strive for is to do all to the glory and honor to God. Always be mindful of Satan's tactics for distracting us from bringing God all the glory. Satan is the master of deception. He may overlook God's work that you are committed to but entice you to give the glory and honor to yourself or someone other than God. Satan may sway the services that we are doing for Christ if we allow it.

When you start feeling overtired, like you're running out of gas, pay attention. Spend some quiet time talking to our Father. God always provides all of the gas we need. If our work is within His will, He will give us that hotshot of gas to make it to the nearby gas station. Never let our indicators go unnoticed. God is always available to refill your tanks and to block the destructive paths of Satan.

CHAPTER 16

DENTIST RECOMMENDATION-
BRUSH A LOT!

Spending time with God and putting Him above all else are two ways to show God how important He is to you. You can also use this technique of spending time to show your partner or children that they are very high on your priority list.

Filter out all the other voices calling your name and trying to control your attention. The voices of distraction come through many different avenues: work, to-do lists, weaknesses, commitments to others, and church. Many times, Christians fall into this trap. God doesn't nag or demand attention. Many times, it's easier to put time with God on the back burner and concede to the loud, outward pulls of attention from the outside.

Quiet time alone with God, submerged in His Word, is essential, but it's not the only time to spend with God. The decision can be made to walk and talk with God not only on Sundays in church or in devotional quiet times but throughout all the craziness of the day.

Some family members are guests; maybe they visit on a holiday or special occasion. You probably take time to be sure your house is in order when they come. You may even dress appropriately (no exercise pants) when they visit. Is God this kind of family guest?

Please don't get me wrong. God loves when you dress up and worship Him at church and offer our services to His godly work here on earth. However, God does not want to be the friend that you only visit when you are ironed and pressed.

Some friends are affectionately called *refrigerator friends*. These are the friends who could walk gallantly into your home unannounced and open the refrigerator and look inside. No one has quite figured out what they look for in there, but still they look. These are the friends with whom you could comfortably sit with in pajamas and drink coffee at any time, day or night. These are friends who could show up at dinnertime when there is no desire or inclination to cook anything for dinner, and that's perfectly fine. These are those friends who may find you down in the dumps, and you haven't even made it to the shower yet. Refrigerator friends know you. They know your interests, likes, dislikes, and they meet you where you are. They know and love the real, raw you.

Anyone who is close to me knows that I own three very special, dogs. These dogs lie on furniture, sleep in various beds at times, and have an essential connection to my heart. As my refrigerator friends are aware, having coffee on my porch is a special treat, but the dogs come as part of the package deal.

God wants to be your "refrigerator friend." He wants to walk with you when you are at your worst—informal, disorganized, scattered state. He wants to be the One whom you come to when you can offer nothing more than sincere thanks for the time He provides to you. He wants to sit in your comfort zones, maybe with your crazy dogs! I say it again—God wants to be your refrigerator friend. He wants to walk with you during every disheveled aspect of every day. God does not want to be only one selected slice of pizza enjoyed on Sunday mornings. He wants to enjoy every slice of your week.

Prayer is a time of calling out to God and talking about what you are thinking, even in all of its ugliness and messiest. God is your best friend. You need to talk to Him about the *stuff* in your life. He doesn't merely want to hear your voice because He's heard your voice many times! He wants to hear about your specific life, your world, your concerns, and your fears. He is not interested in listening to you praying in a callous way for people to view your character.

Prayer is similar to that of a parent whose child is away and calling home. The parent is excited to hear about their child's days, lives, and ups and downs. They do not wish to only hear their child's voice reciting the Pledge of Allegiance.

You may recognize character statements similar to mine when maneuvering through the days of life. It's understandable if you don't want to admit it! The following statements describe my personality. My approach and my ways of thinking are usually the most reasonable ways.

I view myself as a pretty nice person, yet I hate the word *submit.* My hindsight is twenty-twenty. I know what I want, when I want it. I don't like to wait for it. If something is too complicated for me to understand, then I shouldn't feel compelled to know the inner workings. (Of course, my husband, Ron, is the polar opposite, so I lean on him to "figure out" important stuff!)

Many people are experiencing the challenges of talking to God, looking for God's touch, and He doesn't seem to be answering. You know what you want, and you wanted it yesterday. And if you are the dig-deeper personality who needs to know the whys, please research at your own risk!

Pastor Robert Morris of Texas describes praying perfectly. This time of talking with God is like turning on a shower faucet. We wait and wait and wait for the hot water to come when we are getting ready to shower. We wait because we know that the hot water is coming.

However, many times with prayers, Christians start by praying diligently. Then praying stops because no immediate results are seen. Praying is like turning the faucet and waiting for hot water. It won't be immediate, but it will come! If it gets turned off too early, it will not arrive!

Generally, prayer time runs on a schedule, like brushing your teeth. You may say a prayer early in the morning to get a fresh start on the day. You may talk to God again when you eat a meal and again before you fall asleep. Don't get me wrong, it's a good thing to say prayers at those times (it's also good to brush your teeth at those times).

Talking to God is a sure way to get a fresh start on a new day. Prayers at mealtime are important because God always provides. He should be thanked for providing food. Bedtime is also a good prayer time. During the day, a lot of crummy things have happened earlier, and lots of forgiveness is needed!

The issue at hand is that there are a multitude of other things that need prayers! For many Christians, days start off being *behind* before feet even hit the floor. At the end of the day, people are "too pooped to pop." Throughout many days, it seems that you never have two seconds to put together.

So if busy days are already packed until exhaustion at night, how can you possibly add more prayer time? The other potential downfall to the "brush your teeth" prayer schedule is getting caught up in routine words and praying the same old words over and over. The thoughtless routine becomes the norm every day.

> And when you pray, do not keep on babbling like
> pagans, for they think they will be heard because
> of their many words. (Matthew 6:7, NIV)

So to make the Father the King very happy, make it a priority to call home and check in often!

CHAPTER 17

MY "TO-DO" LIST

Refueling while you are waiting for the hot water in prayer is very essential. Make your quiet prayer time the number one priority on your incessant to-do list. Spend scheduled time dedicated solely to God in your personal, warm environment.

Spend a few moments thinking about the environment that best draws you into your quiet time. Make a conscious effort to stick to it. Making this decision ahead of time cuts a lot of unnecessary planning time and distraction away from your precious time. By finding the optimal place to talk with God, all distractions put aside, you will find out how much God has in store for you through your conversations.

The new *normal* gets more and more harried every day. Waiting for anything is not an acceptable option any longer.

Did you know the following facts? *QSR* magazine ("quick-service restaurants") commissioned a study to be done on drive-through wait time at some popular fast-food restaurants. These are the results of their study:

Wendy's	2 minutes, 9 seconds
Taco Bell	2 minutes, 29 seconds
McDonald's	3 minutes, 8 seconds
Chick-fil-A	3 minutes, 10 seconds
Burger King	3 minutes, 20 seconds

Society wants food cooked fresh and hot, money exchanged, and packaged so cars can drive away in less than 3.5 minutes. Waiting is not an accepted option in in a frenzied society anymore.

Take a look at yesterday. How many insignificant things did you find yourself involved in rather than talking with God? (I'm embarrassed to even admit to you, my readers, how much "fluff" time I found in my day.)

Here are some examples of "fluff time" that I identified, and you can add your own personal "fluffs" to the list: catching mindless TV shows, checking social media, listening to the same news story for the third time (yes, the bad news is still the same no matter how many times I watch it!), meandering through a magazine, checking scores, talking on the phone, exercising, and checking e-mails, incessant snacking (healthy or not).

By becoming more productive with your free moments (yes, I said "moments" because in your manic lifestyle, that's how "free time" comes!), then you can carve out a special time with God. You can fill those "insignificant" times with "necessary" times (to eat, wear clean clothes, and pay bills) and still carve out sacred focus time alone with God.

God doesn't expect you to wear dirty laundry or never make your beds. What exactly does the Lord require? As always, the Bible is the treasure map with all of the answers.

> He has made it clear to you, mortal man, what is good. And what the Lord is requiring from you—To act with justice, to treasure the Lord's gracious love, and to walk humbly in the company of your God. (Micah 6:8, ISV)

God asks that you cherish and value His gracious love. Someone that is cherished or highly valued is not put on the back burner, behind a television show, or Social Media.

God asks that Christians act with justice, doing the right thing. (Yes, God is telling you to pay your bills and taxes. Can you fathom saying to the Internal Revenue Service that you are sorry for not paying taxes because you were too busy praying?)

> Let everyone be subject to the governing authorities, for there is no authority except that which God has established. God has established the authorities that exist. Consequently, whomever rebels against the authority is rebelling against what God has instituted, and those who do so will bring judgment on themselves. (Romans 13:1–2, NIV)

God asks for Christians to walk humbly in His company. You will not be able to walk in someone's company if you are not present at all.

Look at your daily schedule. Are you making God your priority or fitting Him into your harried day? Are you not fitting Him in at all? Being *totally* honest, rare and painful, are you guilty of lying to your own self to feel less guilt? Do many things get bumped up in front of prayers? (Some of you, like myself, need all the prayers you can get!)

That negative voice in your head probably reminds you that you experienced a rough day today. You deserve to sit down and put your feet up. Perhaps that familiar voice tells you that God knows what you are thinking anyway, so you really don't need to spend your few precious moments praying.

Listen for God's reminders that the short moments spent in prayer today will enhance tomorrow in ways that are unseen today. You will be surprised as you take notice of your daily schedule and rank the importance of activities. In the bigger picture, are these moments of your day significant?

When frugal parents receive requests from their children, they wisely ask if that request is needed or just wanted. You need to act as those frugal parents, speaking to your inner self. Do you need these moments or just want them? Rid yourself of the dangerous and selfish thought that if you want something, then you should have it.

A lot of fluff time can be shaved or eliminated to give you more control of your time. God is not mandating that you give up all these nonessential times. By examining your time, you are controlling your time instead of letting your time get the best of you.

In your unique lifestyle, when is the optimum time of day for your quiet time? How much time will you need to accomplish the goal of peaceful and unrushed quiet time? By shaving or eliminating time spent in your daily schedule, the harried actions of busy days will be able to fit in around your priority time of prayer.

While evaluating your agenda, you may find that you need to add previously overlooked activities, as well as subtracting the unneeded ones. Take a look at some typical necessities of your time.

After researching exercise, this is the area that I need to add! (Okay, I admit, exercise is not one of the priorities of my day or week or month!) The word is out that exercise is healthy, keeps the weight off, etc. (friends and family who are health nuts have looked disdainfully and said, "Really, you should" And really, I have not!)

The Department of Health and Human Services (HHS) released its new physical activity guidelines for Americans, calling for adults between the ages of eighteen and sixty-four to exercise moderately (such as brisk walking or water aerobics) for at least two hours and thirty minutes or vigorously running, swimming, or cycling (ten miles per hour or faster) for at least an hour and fifteen minutes weekly.

Walking one-half hour per day is manageable, especially if you are a dog owner. Some friends walk together in the early morning before work. The time passes so quickly because they are catching up on family news and still get to work on time.

If your life routine leaves you more strapped for time, a vigorous exercise would only consume fifteen minutes per day. (Yes, I am blessed to own a pool, so why am I always floating on an inner tube? Good question!)

Unfortunately, knowing the recommended guidelines did not propel me to partake. What changed my mind was the amazing health benefits. Exercise is often viewed as an avenue to gain muscle strength and hourglass figures. What is not common knowledge is the fact that exercise can help prevent malicious illnesses. Did you know that many chances of suffering with cancer and diabetes can be prevented with that fifteen or thirty minutes?

Fifteen or thirty minutes of exercise helps the average person to live three to seven years longer by decreasing the risk of major heart issues. William Haskell, a medical professor at Stanford University, stands by this fact. Jonathan Meyers, a health research scientist at the Palo Alto Veterans Affairs Health System in California, states the following fact: "Exercise has a favorable effect on virtually all risk factors of cardiovascular disease."

When a person exercises, the heart muscle contracts forcefully and frequently, increasing blood flow through the arteries. That fifteen or thirty minutes fine-tunes the autonomic nervous system, which controls the contraction and relaxation of these vessels.

Fewer beats to pump blood through the body lower blood pressure, and a more variable heart rate lessens the risk of developing heart disease. All of this transpires because of fifteen or thirty minutes of exercise!

Demetrius Albanes, a researcher at the National Cancer Institute in Bethesda, Maryland, states that regular exercise (yes, there's that fifteen or thirty minutes again) lowers the risk for certain types of cancer, particularly breast and colon cancer. Scientists have not pinpointed the actual reasons for these phenomena, but they are looking at various plausible explanations like circulation of insulin, female hormones, and increased immune systems. Granted, healthier lifestyles play a part in this connection between exercise and lowering risk for disease.

Moderate exercise increases and maintains bone mass and reduces the risk of the bone disease osteoporosis. Bone-fracture risk is much greater if the fifteen or thirty minutes of exercise is not practiced.

I need to hear things plain and simple—not in highly scientific, genius mentality and medical terms, as you well know from walking with me through this book.

Fifteen or thirty minutes of exercise can prevent you from going through the war zone of heart problems and cancer. Those extra moments added on to your lifespan are valuable moments of quiet time with God that You would gain.

My *most* wasteful fluff-time is the false god of food and snacking. A false god is anything that we put before God, either unintentionally or intentionally. I'm not just talking about unhealthy snacking of potato chips and cookies. Health addictions can act the same way.

All right, time for brutal and painful honesty. What do you think about most? There are many addictions alive in our world like drug and alcohol addictions. Addiction means craving, need, compulsion, and obsession.

A large portion of my time is spent thinking about food. What would I like to fix for dinner? What am I going to eat when we go to that restaurant this weekend? I can't make it to the cashier in a grocery store without skimming through the recipe booklets layered neatly above the candy bars. Food is my most time-consuming fluff. I can't remember the last time I ate merely to survive. It's like a vacation time for me: I plan it, look forward to it, and wallow in it. Here's the clincher to prove my addiction: I get downright grouchy ("hangry") when I have to wait or the plans change.

So how can this food addict erase fluff time and add quality time with God? (I am a work in progress just like you! I'll let you know when I figure it out.)

By shaving and consolidating our time, we have more control over the moments of free time that we have. Invite God to interact personally during your activity. Listen to a favorite Christian singer or speaker while on a treadmill. Snack while going on a "prayer" walk.

Check into Christian groups who post on Facebook where one can talk with others to stimulate Christian lives. Set a time limit for indulging in nonproductive fluff times. Make a conscious effort to watch only one news report and two mindless television shows per night. By doing this and sticking to it, you will be amazed at the "free" time that suddenly appears!

Listen. Quietly, you may hear the applause from heaven when you flop down to celebrate your quiet time.

CHAPTER 18

CAFÉ AU LAIT

Having a conversation with our Father is the link connecting our relationship with Him. You've examined your days and realized how much fluff time" you can rid your life of to put your priorities where they belong. God is our center, and everything revolves around Him.

God created all people with unique different personalities. Prayer time reflects on those differences. Fingerprints show how unique God created you. Millions and millions of fingerprint records have been analyzed. No two duplicate fingerprint patterns have ever been recorded. Ever. A human fetus begins having a unique set of fingerprints developed during his or her three-month gestation mark. Probably from their placement in the womb, even identical twins have different fingerprints from each other. Christians were created differently from the very beginning.

> For You created my inmost being; You knit me together in my mother's womb... Your eyes saw my unformed body; all the days ordained for me were written in Your book before one of them came to be. (Psalm 139:13, 16, NIV)

God created every small thread of who you are. Saint Augustine, a well-known Catholic priest, said, "God loves each of us as if there were only one of us." Each is not only unique but also adored and cherished by our Lord.

Creation of individuals and not robots results in prayer and worship, affecting Christians in different ways. To learn the best fit of worship and praise for your unique personality starts by self-honesty. View yourself as if you were watching yourself play a character on a TV sitcom. How would your character fit into different worship settings?

Praying is sort of like drinking a beverage. (Isn't it funny how easily things are put into a food or drink context?) "Earl tea prayers" like to have a nice cup of tea with their silverware and dishes properly set. Usually their dinners and tea are routinely regimented and oriented. They prefer the same time, the same place, rain or shine, day after day, and year after year. These church members savor regimented, old-fashioned traditions. They are content and comfortable following past traditions. "Earls" do not like any change to their routines. The environment is also very important to them. They like order and probability.

As faithfully as they savor and enjoy a cup of tea, you would never see Earls grabbing a carryout cup of tea from a neighborhood coffee shop. Earls prefer traditional prayers in a routine setting. They prefer reciting those prayers in a group. Requests to pray randomly aloud would be answered with silence or flashes of extreme embarrassment. An Earl member once told me that she was a member of the "frozen chosen group" that never worshipped or prayed in any freestyle way. Prayers from the hearts of Earls are certainly as precious to God as loud Spirit-filled personal prayers lifted by another Christian.

Where can Earls effectively spend precious private time with God? Earls need to find a comfortable spot where love for routine will not be constantly challenged. On a bus, with constant interruptions, while traveling to work would probably not be an optimum spot for an Earl. They prefer routine and order. Consistency, privacy, and completion are a must.

Choose a time of day to be devoted to your prayer time. Pick a time when you have time to follow your consistent routine components from start to finish. Earls do not like open-ended, unfinished routines. Distraction and disturbance send them into the red zone!

Although preferring traditional prayers, Earls like to relate those prayers to their unique lives. Making a formal prayer personal is acceptable in solace to Earls.

> Our Father, who art in heaven,
> hallowed be Thy name.
> Thy kingdom come,
> Thy will be done, on earth as it is in heaven (Your will, Lord, not mine).
> Give us this day our daily bread (provide for my family).
> Forgive us our trespasses (my sins),
> as we forgive those who trespass against us (unpleasant action done to me).
> Deliver us from evil (my bad habits, temptations, shortcomings).
> For Thine is the kingdom, the power, and the glory forever and ever, amen.

Unknowingly, you are probably very familiar with Earl and his published works. Earl was probably one of the "anonymous" authors who wrote the formal prayers that we have ingrained in our minds through the years!

How many times have you recited, "God is so good, God is so great. Let us thank Him for the food we eat"? Or, "Come, Lord Jesus, be our guest. Let this food to us be blessed"? Your life would feel incomplete without the visible and unique touches of Earls.

"Herbals" prefer the natural teas. They enjoy different varieties and like to change their desired choice as long as it stays within the realm of natural and wholesome qualities. The Herbals feel the most comfortable in natural surroundings, without any manufactured or confining ingredients. They sip slowly, savor the natural, and feel the outdoor fragrances stirring up their inner souls.

When they are put in a very regimented environment with rules and regulations, their creative souls feel stifled and stagnant. Herbals are whimsical and carefree. They like to be involved in sporadic and unplanned moments. They tend to be inviting, welcoming, and very nonjudgmental.

How can prayers be more meaningful for Herbals? Dedicate a certain time of the day to prayer time. Find a comfortable spot for feeling God's presence the most. Herbals' prayers might be felt most effectively on a hike in a forest, on sands of a quiet beach, or a calm porch with the sound of birds, music, or raindrops in the background. They might feel a great longing, yet peace, under a vast night sky of twinkling stars. Herbals like to surround themselves with the wonders of God's creation. With every sip, they take in and appreciate His majestic power and beauty.

They free their minds to travel anywhere they want in prayer. The gentle sounds of nature free them from any stress or worries of the moment. They lift their spirits unashamedly to listen and to worship the Creator of it all. The Herbals are filled with musicians writing songs that are inspired by nature. Some family members are clergy who write their best sermons after talking with God, on a long walk, or hearing the waves.

"Blacks" are very hardworking, dedicated, no-frills, and frugal. Blacks defend their beliefs wholeheartedly with innately strong faiths. After a long, hard day of work, they are gracious and willing to thank God in appreciation for the multitude of blessings in their lives. Blacks thrive in an environment filled with down-to-earth and practical components.

They comfortably roll their sleeves up and lift requests for the tools needed to get a job completed. Blacks thank God for supplying those resources. Their prayers tend to be predominantly "black-and-white" rather than ideological. Prayers often contain practical requests for a doctor's touch, money to pay bills, or jobs to be found.

Blacks are willing to follow God's leading and serve. Without requests, they offer any possible help they can give. Acts of service for God, combined with their practical and down-to-earth natures, make them very valuable assets in active Christian environments.

How can Blacks maximize their prayer time? A casual and solid environment should be located for time for prayer. Boundaries for Blacks themselves and others need to be arranged at the commencement. A standing order is clearly laid out that no petty tasks, work projects, or distractions, may appear during this quiet time. No picking up clutter, answering a phone, organizing a pile of papers nearby, answering an e-mail, checking a score, changing laundry around can be done. Close friends and family will come to understand Blacks' commitment and change their expectations for Blacks to respond during this sacred time.

Keeping a prayer journal is a nice asset for Blacks, who gain satisfaction by keeping lists and checking things off. They enjoy writing specific prayer requests on the list. The die-hard Blacks will even write something on a list they are compiling even if that prayer has already been answered just so they can check it off! Blacks will serve in any capacity that they are able. They would give the shirt off their backs if someone needed one while thanking God that they were blessed with the shirt to give!

"Café To-gos" are high-paced, multitasking Christians. It may appear to others that they are often harried in their fast pace. Actually, the To-gos thrive at this pace. They feel most comfortable with time deadlines rather than open and timeless relaxation.

To-gos would not be located in a remote "no cell signal" or "no Wi-Fi" location, quietly sitting in a Jacuzzi alone for an extended vacation. To-gos would be the members who would organize and invite people to a get together and entertain around a Jacuzzi. Their engines are powered by being around other people. They run full throttle until they collapse in bed at the end of the day.

How can To-gos find time in their hurried lives for prioritizing God? Find an active Christian environment where there is great activity and interaction with people. Megachurches or large prayer meetings are environments where To-gos thrive. The busyness and constant motions don't distract them; they empower them!

To-gos need to feel successful in an area before feeling empowered. Once they get a taste of success, they would feel exuberant sharing prayer times with others, outwardly and vocally. To-gos are vital parts of our churches' growths. They outwardly embrace the more timid personalities. Those quiet souls who are blessed to cross paths with To-gos are encouraged to increase their involvement and step out of natural comfort zones.

One downfall for To-gos is burning out in the high-energy department and letting their own active prayer lives die out. Often, these high-paced Christians are so outward at focusing on others, helping others to strengthen their faiths, that they don't focus enough on their own personal prayers. Their own needs are overlooked, and prayer time diminishes. To-gos need to ensure that they don't act so frenzied that they reach a place where they're "get up and go, got up and went!"

To-gos face a danger in getting too caught up in the excitement of the moment and forgetting to center their energies on God Himself. By engaging in an active prayer time directed toward their own lives, God will reenergize and refresh their active souls.

"Cappuccino Lattes" are stylish, fashionable, and trendy. They like color, pizazz, excitement, and high fashion. Owning and working with all the bells and whistles is very desirable to them. The Cappuccino Lattes show deep appreciation to God for the appearances of blessings that clearly come from Him.

Cappuccino Lattes do not believe in doing something without putting the time and effort into making it turn out successfully. Whatsoever their hands are involved with come out beautifully designed and well-orchestrated. These are the Christians who can be thanked for wonderfully designed worship services. The sound system is top-of-the-line, and the ambiance is impeccable. The floral arrangements are stylish. The Narthex to the church is stylish, fashionable, and welcoming. There may be coffee and Danishes in place.

Prayer lives can be more meaningful and productive if Cappuccino Lattes schedule quiet prayer time in an environment where they are comfortable. By nature, they are very observant about styles and atmospheres. The ambiance cannot not retract from the experience. They thrive in places that are modern and well updated.

Cappuccino Lattes enjoy comforts like heat and air-conditioning. They would be extremely distracted in an old-style environment filled with items needing fixing. Components like aroma, seating, temperature, and lighting must be pleasing. They would not have a good prayer time on a park bench outside on a warm afternoon. Their innately strong conversations with God would be best activated on a comfortable chair in a fashionable, air-conditioned environment.

To create the most productive and fruitful prayer experience, look at yourself honestly and figure out what kind of environment makes you feel energized and connected with God. Churches can accommodate many different worship and prayer types on the church property to allow different worship styles to truly gain a meaningful worship and prayer experience.

Satan sends enough of his own distractions during our active prayer time. Teach yourself to surround yourself with the environment where Satan has the least grounds to use. Our natural comfort zones will help to curb his efforts.

When you find that place that makes you feel energized and open, make a standing date with the Lord. He will meet you there!

You have found the most peaceful and optimum place to pray. Do you know what to say when you get there?

CHAPTER 19

ROARING 20's

G reat family recipes are baked from scratch (an honorable delicious talent that I never acquired!). Prayers are very similar. One family scratch recipe I will never forget is the recipe for prayer. Travel with me through the world of ingredients of this family recipe made easily understandable through a basic, simple acronym: PRAY = praise, repent, ask, yield.

In the chapters ahead, you will look at each essential ingredient of this precious family recipe. But for now, you are going to glance over the recipe to see which ingredients you need and which ingredients you already have on hand.

> Praise the LORD. How good it is to sing praises to our God, how pleasant and fitting to praise him! Serve the Lord with gladness; come before His presence with singing. (Psalm 100:2)

Music is very important to God. This fact is very visible in the Bible. David felt this feeling of strong connection with God, so 73 of the 150 psalms in the Hebrew Bible are attributed to King David. Music is also used in the heavenly realms for worshipping God.

Many Bible scholars believe that Satan was the angel delegated for worship. The name *Lucifer* means "day star" or "son of the morning." Lucifer was created perfect in beauty and wisdom. He did not have a plain or ordinary appearance and was covered with gold and precious stones. He was a step above the other angels and held a very

high standing in his job serving God in heaven whose ministry sur-
rounded the heart of heaven.

God created him like all other angels. However, his role was different from the others. Lucifer was referred to as the "covering angel."
Angels who were assigned to this detail were specially anointed. One
such special cherub covered the mercy seat of the Ark of the Cove-
nant with his wings. Needless to say, whether Lucifer was the "angel
of worship" or "the protector of the throne." Lucifer was indeed a
very close servant to God (pretty substantial job, no?).

> You were in Eden, the garden of God; every pre-
> cious stone adorned you: carnelian, chrysolite
> and emerald, topaz, onyx and jasper, lapis lazuli,
> turquoise and beryl. Your settings and mountings
> were made of gold; on the day you were created
> they were prepared. (Ezekiel 28:13, NIV)

Timbrel and pipes built were created within him from the
beginning.

> The workmanship of your timbrels and pipes was
> prepared for you on the day you were created.
> You were the anointed cherub who covers and
> protects, And I placed you there. You were on the
> holy mountain of God; You walked in the midst
> of the stones of fire [sparkling jewels]. (Ezekiel
> 28:14, AMP)

There are many ways to offer praise to God. One avenue for
offering praise is through music. This forum can be done in many
different desired genres. If your love is for country music with banjos,
guitars, and harmonicas, there are many choices for country music
worship songs.

If your genre of choice is hard rock music, Southern gospel, contemporary, or big-band music, do a simple search, and worship songs

are not hard to find. With technology the way it stands today, taking music with you to any environment is possible and easily accessible.

Timbrels (or tabrets) were the main musical instruments of percussion of the Israelites. Timbrels were similar to modern tambourines. Pipes refer to tubes used to produce tones by blowing air through them, like within an organ. Many scholars believe that Lucifer had the makings of percussion instruments and wind instruments built into his very being. Presently, he does not use them to bring glory to God but to turn God's creatures against Him. Satan is still visible in the powerful influence through music today.

Music is an important way to draw close to God while praising Him. This is also another avenue that can be used against the wiles of Satan. You can hum Christian songs by memory through your day. By doing this, you are surrounding yourself with God's presence. Be aware of techniques that Satan still uses to maneuver these talents that God created him with. The influence is substantial, especially in teenagers, even subconsciously. Be mindful of the music playing within your home and cars.

Praising God with words is a powerful aspect of worship.

> Therefore by Him let us continually offer sacrifice of praise to God, that is, the fruit of our lips, giving thanks to His name. (Hebrews 13:15)

Language is a very powerful and valuable tool that places humans above all other creatures. The gallant road map, the Bible, has numerous passages on the power of words. God lays the answers out for those focusing on improving the *praise* part of prayer life. How can words be offered to God as praise besides singing the lyrics to Christian praise songs?

Invite God to be present while walking through every small part of your day. It truly is astonishing how many blessings are taken for granted and not acknowledged. When showering in the morning, cooking dinner, or washing the car, do you notice that the water comes right to you with the turn of a handle? When complaining about an unkempt house, is thanksgiving lifted for the warm or cool home filled with all the extra belongings that cause a house to be unkempt? When hurriedly doing piles of laundry and complaining about mismatched socks, is God offered a prayer of thanksgiving for giving socks and underwear? When cleaning out refrigerators, is God thanked and praised for families being well nourished (in fact, *too* well-nourished)?

Days filled with blessings from God are so close Christians trip over them, and yet God does not hear praise and thanksgiving. So next time you are doing chores and feeling unappreciated, smile at yourself as you can almost hear God saying He knows how you feel!

Words are a very powerful way to praise God for sure. However, God delights in praise also by subtracting words. The definition of *praise* is "thanks, approval, and admiration." Sometimes words must be erased for these gifts to be offered as praise.

> You shall not use or repeat the name of the Lord
> your God in vain [that is, lightly or frivolously,
> in false affirmations or profanely]: for the Lord
> will not hold him guiltless who takes His name
> in vain. (Exodus 20:7, AMPC)

Someone's name would not be run through the mud if they were truly admired. If something occurred to make you steam with anger, would you then telephone and berate a close friend? Subtraction of a negative tongue is often needed to ensure pain and evil are not substituting for a loving heart. Speaking aloud is like squirting ketchup on a hot dog. Once the ketchup comes out of the bottle, it is out. Words are the same. Once vocalized, they cannot be put back inside and left unsaid. When hitting the air, they are out in the open and cannot return. A familiar old saying goes reminds to think before you speak. Make sure that those words spoken are acceptable to be heard and remembered for a lifetime. By curbing your tongue, you are actually praising God.

"Let go and let God" means releasing your grip on a situation and allowing God the room needed to handle it. After all, He is our trusted Protector in every challenging situation! It makes God happy also when we are with other believers and praising Him in fellowship.

> I will declare Your name to My brethren; in the
> midst of the assembly I will sing praise to You.
> (Hebrews 2:12)

Parents really enjoy seeing their children fellowshipping with one another and not killing one another. The cherry on the top is if they are fellowshipping together and talking about what great parents they have. My youngest daughter with four-year-old priceless wisdom told me that she knew why brothers and sisters fight with one another: it's God's way of keeping them from getting married! (Through the mouths of babes!)

God too also is very fond of seeing His children fellowshipping and chatting about how great their Father is!

> Lift up your hands in the sanctuary, and bless the
> Lord. (Psalm 134:2)

> Let them praise His name with the dance; let
> them sing praises to Him with the timbrel and
> harp. (Psalm 149:3)

Lift up your hands in the sanctuary. Many Christians love to lift their hands during worship or dance. But for many Christians, lifting their hands and dancing in worship is an out-of-character and uncomfortable way for them to praise God.

Sanctuary means "holy place." Do you think that God specifies church as the only sanctuary? A holy place is a place where God is present.

Lifting your hands can mean doing act of service. Timbrels and harps are instruments which could also be tools. Praising God could be felt during acts of service, which may include hammering, baking, painting, laying brick, or crocheting. As long as we make that environment a "holy place," God will meet us there.

Praising God can be visible by giving a small gift to another as a sign of thanks to God for blessing us with that person in your life. "Have-a-nice-day" gifts are very small and inexpensive ways to let someone know that you are thinking of them and care for them. The gifts are personal to the one you are acknowledging and thanking for being a part of your life. A perfect example is if I have a very close friend who loves elephants. If I should stumble across an elephant tea towel or a heartwarming story about an elephant, it may become a have-a-nice-day gift, unexpectedly. It's personal; it's not generic. If I gave someone else an elephant, they would probably smile in a civil way and think I was more off base than I already am!

Like our close friends, God doesn't require Have-a-nice-day gifts at any time. What does God ask of us?

> And now, Israel, what does the Lord your God ask of you but to fear the Lord your God, to walk in obedience to him, to love him, to serve the Lord your God with all your heart and with all your soul. (Deuteronomy 10:12, NIV)

By reading this book, you trying to strengthen your life, one surface at a time. So take a good look at each area of what God requires of us. If improvements in each area can be made, God will bless you, and your life can only improve. Sounds pretty easy, right?

The Hebrew verb *yare* means "to fear, to respect, to reverence." Fear of God is an attitude of respect, a response of reverence and wonder. It is the only appropriate response to our Creator and Redeemer (Nelson's NKJV Study Bible 1997).

> The fear of the Lord is the beginning of knowledge, but fools despise wisdom and instruction. (Proverbs 1:7, NIV)

> The fear of the Lord is the beginning of wisdom; All who follow his precepts have good under-

standing. To him belongs eternal praise. (Psalm 111:10, NIV)

What have-a-nice-day gifts could I unexpectedly give to Him to show Him my faithfulness? I can't surprise God because He already knows everything. It's more of an unexpected surprise for me that I am offering a token of my thanks, unplanned, to my best friend.

What have-a-nice-day gifts could I possibly give to God? Help another person with grocery-store trips, shovel snow for an elderly church member, give an extra ten minutes during your busy day to spend with God, resist a temptation, lift an unexpected prayer of thanksgiving.

Dictionary.com describes word *praise* as "the act of expressing approval or admiration; commendation; laudation, the offering of grateful homage in words or song, as an act of worship: a hymn of praise to God... to express approval or admiration of; commend; extol."

Let everything that has breath praise the Lord. (Psalm 150:6)

When you do something nice or make a good choice, acknowledge to yourself that you are, in fact, lifting a have-a-nice-day gift to God. You are worshipping Him and showing Him how important He is in your heart.

Chapter 20

"I did it my Way"
Duel to the Death

Repenting is another ingredient needed for the special recipe of prayer that is truly needed to make your work complete. In this chapter, the essential ingredient is hopefully going to be located by visiting the special Frank Sinatra "resort of repentance."

Christians were given free choice from the beginning, so good or bad decisions are made by your own admission. Sinful nature overtakes righteous nature many, many times (like nine hundred plus times?). It's usually fairly easy to realize that I have committed a sin. Reflecting about the mistake is not easy. *Admitting* the bad decision and asking with a heavy heart to erase the mistake? Well, that's a different story.

If you are a flawless individual, then you probably should skip over this chapter. If you *think* you are flawless for the majority of your time, you should stay put for this chapter. If you are similar to myself and look in the mirror and wonder how it is possible to screw up so many times in such a short amount of time (*Guinness Book of World Records* is attempting to reach us), then you are in the right place!

Repentance is asking for forgiveness for the sins that were committed. God clearly laid out the rules, the Ten Commandments, to follow in Exodus 20. Falling short of these commandments is sin. The only way to erase mistakes is to repent by asking God to forgive.

Ready? Did you pack a flashlight, a drink, and a box of Kleenex? (I have a feeling that you may need them, as I did, on this trip!) Let the adventures begin!

You are greeted at the door when you arrive. The man warmly welcomes you to this fine establishment. Someone has communicated with him that you are weary and need relief from that heavy load you've been carrying (how does he know your load is so heavy?). He points out the many places you will see will be pretty dark when first entering because you are unfamiliar with that place. Don't be anxious about the darkness; you will find light. You will surely run into the owner while visiting. He's kind, strong, and well-known for gladly assisting in carrying heavy loads. Smiling, the man sends you on your way.

An intriguing castle is nestled in the hills. Although heavy, your backpack is fastened on pretty snuggly. It is filled with poor choices, sinful ways, hurt, regret, misunderstandings, anger, resentment, and bitterness. You would love to lighten this load like the advertisements promise. Continuing along a wooded path, birds are singing, crickets are chirping, and a gentle breeze is rustling leaves in the massive trees. It's so beautiful that, for occasional moments, you don't mind laying down the heavy backpack to rest.

Through the clearing and up ahead, the massive stone castle with circular turrets is peeking up above nearby trees. One of the entrances shows a hand-carved sign above that reads, "Edison Place—Home of Thoughts and Ideas."

A man with a battered brow and warm smile approaches. He reaches out his gentle hand and takes the heavy backpack. His gentle voice is quiet and calming. There are many unique rooms to explore. He'll be close by if you ever need Him or to sort through your bags. He will carry them until you wish to carry them. Many rooms? Yikes! This must be the owner that the front desk was speaking about. Words cannot even show the amount of gratitude you are feeling to be freed of the heavy bag. As the cherry on top, he will be available for questions along the way!

The first room will looks and feels somewhat familiar, even though you have never been there before. Across the room, a charming table with bent legs is visible with a lamp. A book lies open on the table. The first page will be labeled with your full name. (Is Michael Carbonaro, the magician, behind this? Are you soon to be an unwitting contestant on *The Carbonaro Effect* show?)

The kind owner will pat you on the shoulder. He will tell you of many photographs that you may recognize from earlier times. He welcomes you to stay as long as you wish and will graciously offer the comfortable chair to browse through the book. There is no rush. Curiosity and intrigue, with a twinge of nervousness, flow through your mind. Remember, you are on a quest to find the special ingredient of repentance for the family recipe of prayer life. Could this book hold any clues?

The worn and tattered book is filled with watermark backgrounds of faded pictures of family, friends, and acquaintances from your life. In some pictures, you will recognize faces, but the names will surely escape you (names escaping you—who'd have thought?). You will realize that you must have spent time with these people at some point because you are present in each photo. There will also be pictures of strangers standing with you throughout this unusual book.

Peek your head out and ask the gentleman why this book filled with pictures of your life is in this room at all. His response will be that all the people on these pages are people whom you have hurt in some way through the years. I'm sure you will experience the same incredulous look plastered on my face as I felt when I traveled through this room.

What? How can that be possible? You don't even know some of these people! You are a kind and decent person, and you are rarely malicious! You'll find some familiar words coming to your lips. "Lord, I don't understand. Why would someone make a book like this?" As usual, you will turn to God for guidance and direction. You will find yourself asking for some clarity.

You probably will barely get the prayer out of your mouth when the kind man will poke his head in the door. Listen closely to his direction as he'll probably suggest looking through the book. By looking at the pictures, you may gain more insight. Take as long as you need. He will not leave you while you try to figure things out.

Leaf through the book; it probably won't be a slim booklet. The books are divided up into sections of sins against God, sins against others, sin against yourself. Some sins are intentional. Poor decisions were made, even though that little voice nudged you deeply inside that this action was wrong. Words, actions, physical injury, hurt feelings, prideful thoughts, and the list goes on and on. If feelings of guilt washed over, they were probably too late, and the sin could not be taken back.

Some sins were unintentional. The actions or words were intentional; there was very little thought far enough ahead. The long-lasting effects that actions may have are not considered before they are committed. The effects can be felt in families, workplaces, social lives, and even churches. Trust is lost when promises and commitments are not followed through. Trust that is lost will lead to insecurity, resentment, mistrust, anger, and pain. The long-lasting effects spill over into many different areas.

Words are sometimes more cutting than actions. Misunderstandings, disappointments, and questioning self-worth can follow comments. Criticism can often leave a lifetime scar. The scars, especially caused by people one is closest to, can affect a whole life. Parents can affect a child's self-esteem with words. In turn, those children grow up to be parents and affect their own children. The trickle-down effect of words and actions is immense. These sins that get passed down through the lines usually go unnoticed and not repented for.

It's painful to think that sins, bad decisions, words affected others in such negative ways. Repentance is needed for the hurt that is caused.

I'm so sorry, Lord, for all the many hurts that I caused. Please help me to be mindful of my words and callous actions. Help me to be a vessel for You and pass on kindness instead of pain.

Sins against self are often minimized because Christians feel it's all right to do anything to your own self. Actions or words that are obviously wrong toward God or toward others are viewed as sinful, but when was the last time you asked for repentance for words or actions you did to yourself?

God created you so any pain directed at yourself is a sin toward God.

> Do you not know that your body is a temple of the Holy Spirit who is within you, whom you have [received as a gift] from God, and that you are not your own [property]? (1 Corinthians 6:19, AMP)

Addictions and sexual promiscuity are the two most common sins to be related with misusing God's temple in the body. There are many sins committed against the self that are probably not even viewed as sins.

So why is repentance so important? Before Jesus, Christians were held accountable to the *laws of Moses*. Almost every aspect of Old Testament life was covered under these strict components of the laws. The *Ten Commandments* covered many of the moral laws like murder, theft, honesty, adultery. *Food laws* covered clean and unclean cooking and storing food. *Feast laws* covered special occasions: the Day of Atonement, Passover, Feast of Tabernacles, Feast of Unleavened Bread, Feast of Weeks. *Purity laws* dealt with personal issues: menstruation, seminal emissions, skin disease, mildew. *Social laws* covered issues with property, inheritance, marriage, and divorce. Sacrifices and offerings were required for sins, thanks, feasts, peace, and tithes of firstfruits.

Leviticus 20 covers of the actions or punishments a person would be inflicted with who was found guilty of not following these laws. Death caused by crucifying, stoning, burning, beheading, strangling, and even drowning was the most prevalent punishment. By default, you would have faced death for any of the following: hitting or reviling a parent, profanity, not going to church on Sunday, adultery, witchcraft, having sex before marriage, rape, or kidnapping. Would Christians of today ever survived past the age of ten?

Secondary punishments might be "an eye for an eye," thirty lashes, scourging with briars and thistles, being imprisoned, being humiliated, or evicted forever from the community.

Why did Jesus die on the cross? He took ownership of all the bad decisions and the death sentences that would follow. Imagine that you were next in line, waiting your turn in the electric chair. A decent, innocent man voluntarily took your place in line and accepted the punishment that followed.

Jesus did this for Christians. Now, justified, just because of faith in Him, Christians don't have to face these death sentences. After making hundreds of bad decisions in a day, Christians are able to apologize and get another chance.

Imagine how innocent Jesus must feel because the majority of times, no apology is even offered to Him. Excuses or denial occur rather than remorse for the sin that put Him in that position in the first place.

> Clearly no one who relies on the law is justi-fied before God, because "the righteous will live by faith." The law is not based on faith; on the contrary, it says, "The person who does these things will live by them." Christ redeemed us from the curse of the law by becoming a curse for us, for it is written: "Cursed is everyone who is hung on a pole." He redeemed us in order that the blessing given to Abraham might come to the Gentiles through Christ Jesus, so that by faith we might receive the promise of the Spirit. (Galatians 3:11–14, NIV)

While paging through your booklet, you may feel your face getting hot with embarrassment as you realize, as I realized, all the infractions and pain that you inflicted. Those memories may flash before your eyes.

Overall, your self-assessment shows a relatively honest person. However, according to this book, blatant dishonesty occurred time and time again. What could possibly cause dishonesty with God, with others, and self? Even while glancing through these pages showing dis-honesty, the temptation still nudges to make excuses for these sins.

The memories, like snapshots, come flashing back. With all these false statements tucked away in the recesses of the mind, it's amazing that other thoughts are not completely blocked. The list of unfulfilled promises, criticisms, selfishness, greed, jealous jabs, bitterness, and disloyalty goes on and on. Responsibility for these sins is yours because you were not forced to commit them.

Play back the words of the confession that you say every week. It feels much different now. The guilt is up close and personal. These wrongdoings are not lumped together in a casual confession. These are individual cases where you let God, others, and yourself down. You feel the hurt that was caused. You see the sins committed firsthand in this book.

Do you want to remain the sin-filled person represented in your book? The great news for Christians is that, by justification, they are saved. By saying a prayer of repentance, all these sins will be cleared away forever, never to be seen again.

> Lord, I confess to You that I have done these wrongs. I am so sorry that I caused these horribly painful things. I know I deserve my rightful punishment in return for my actions. Lord, I truly understand now how deep Your mercy and love are for me. I don't deserve Your kindness and goodness. Please forgive me.

Words of apology come, and a few drops of tears fall. The kind owner peeks his head back in the doorway. Smiling, he returns the backpack. The bag is now lightweight and empty. Amazingly, you feel like you are walking on a cloud. The heaviness and regrets have disappeared. The feelings of anger and resentment have disappeared. Feeling like a new person, ready to walk confidently and openly, you are now ready to continue on your journey.

CHAPTER 21

ASKING FOR J-O-Y (JESUS-OTHERS, YOURSELF)

The facts so far are much clearer now. You praise God because you know what a hot mess you are and how many tangles He gets you through. You would not be able to survive a single day without His touch. Truly, He is the best friend, confidant, and strength that you will ever need. You have been convicted of the quantity and magnitude of terrible things committed. Repentance has provided a clean slate and new start.

God welcomes requests for things that your heart desires. Numerous times, God gives the welcoming invitation to ask Him for anything.

Hopefully, the set-apart, special devotional time with God has now been established. The significance of this time of praising and giving thanks is immense in any Christian faith walk. It is crystal clear how incredible God is and how low and sinful Christians are. In that process, God has shown how deep and wide His mercy and love must be to lighten the heavy load of sins with such a sacrifice. He is the friend to curl up with, looking as you do, before drinking coffee. Don't perform or recite, just surround yourself with His presence and see where He leads.

So now what should you add to your quiet time of prayer? He invites you to ask Him anything. The stage opens wide to pray for many others, family, friends, and people you know or even strangers.

Ask and it will be given to you; seek and you
will find; knock and the door will be opened to
you. For everyone who asks receives; the one who
seeks finds; and to the one who knocks, the door
will be opened. (Matthew 7:7–8, NIV)

Healing for others is probably the most common thread in our
prayers for others. Jesus was known as the healer. People flocked to
Him in hopes of His touch or words for healing. Seven hundred and
twenty-four verses out of 3,779 verses in the four gospels relate spe-
cifically to the healing of physical and mental illness and the resurrection of the dead. "The attention devoted to the healing ministry of
Jesus is far greater than that devoted to any one kind of experience"
(Gary Wiens, "The Healing Ministry of Jesus," International House
of Prayer Northwest)

Worship the Lord your God, and his blessing will
be on your food and water. I will take away sick-
ness from among you. (Exodus 23:25, NIV)

Lord my God, I called to you for help, and you
healed me. (Psalm 30:2, NIV)

Jesus healed the sick, like the lepers, blind, deaf, and paralyzed.
Today many life-threatening illnesses are faced as well. My greatest
hope as the author is that in my lifetime, the cure for cancer will be
discovered.

Jesus didn't heal rich and famous to make a name for Himself.
He healed the abandoned, the outsiders, the rejected, and the sinners. Thankfully, He still reaches out to the average and common
folk. I am living proof of that!

God healed me from a traumatic brain injury years ago from a
bad car accident. I was in a coma with tracheotomy for three weeks,
hospital and feeding tube for months. My mode of transportation
was a wheelchair and walker for months. I should not have been able
to shower and dress myself, but I do. I should not have been able to

cook a meal or feed myself, but I do. I should not have been able to ever drive or work again, but I do. I should not have been able to write words on a page again, but I do. You are sharing in my miracle of healing right now.

Within the last week, you have probably prayed for the physical healing of at least two people. However, healing doesn't have to be restricted to physical needs. Emotional turmoil can be just as devastating as physical issues, both for that person and those who are in close contact with that person.

There is a vast illness that troubles our homes, our country, and our churches called depression. This illness is often wrongly attributed to families, work conditions, life circumstances, stress, or losses. Waking up on the wrong side of the bed, finding yourself in a funk, or experiencing down days are familiar to all who wake up in the morning.

Perhaps you have experienced the loss of a loved one or job. You've been left with such stress and sadness that you feel like there will never be light at the end of this tunnel of gloom. King David felt this type of sadness:

> Be merciful to me, O Lord, for I am in distress; my eyes grow weak with sorrow, my soul and my body with grief. My life is consumed by anguish and my years by groaning; my strength fails because of my affliction, and my bones grow weak. I am forgotten by them as though I were dead. (Psalm 31:9–10, 12)

As desperate as these conditions seem, a time will come when the darkness is lifted. This emotional sad state differs from clinical depression, which does not lift when conditions improve. Clinical depression can be caused by a change in brain activity. There is decreased activity in the left frontal lobe during depression. After the brain activity is stabilized, the levels rise again. Overactive and underactive regions of the brain are at the biological cause of major depressive disorder.

The release of neurotransmitters (serotonin, norepinephrine, and dopamine) in the brain is also linked to depression. It is very difficult to measure the concentrations of these neurotransmitters in the brain. The connection is seen because antidepressant drugs have reactions to the neurotransmitters that stabilize the depression.

Depression cannot be diagnosed because a person is in sad mood and a lack of interest is visible. If that were the case, everyone would be diagnosed with clinical depression! Sad mood and lack of interest has to be accompanied with four of the following symptoms over a two-week period: "feelings of worthlessness or inappropriate guilt, diminished ability to concentrate or make decisions, fatigue, inability to sit still, incessantly just sitting around, not sleeping, sleeping too much, significant decrease or increase in appetite or weight, reoccurring thoughts of death or suicide."

Clinical depression is not just a negative state of mind or a result from how stress is handled. True clinical depression can affect someone in physical ways as well. Common side effects include difficulty focusing, erratic sleep habits, change in appetite, constant fatigue, muscle aches, headaches, and back pain. The person suffering from clinical depression usually suffers a double-whammy emotional and physical pain.

Prayer for lightening of this load is needed for those who suffer in this way. While saying this prayer, try not to focus on the misconceptions of what could be causing this person's sadness. Pray instead for the load to be lightened or taken away.

Jesus healed His good friend Lazarus, bringing him back to life. He intentionally waited until after Lazarus's death so that the people around would see that miracles can happen through God. If Jesus had come earlier, some would think that Lazarus felt better and it wasn't God sending the healing.

> Father, I thank you that you have heard me. I knew that you always hear me, but I said this for the benefit of the people standing here, that they may believe that you sent me. When he had said this, Jesus called in a loud voice, "Lazarus, come

out!" The dead man came out, his hands and feet wrapped with strips of linen, and a cloth around his face. Jesus healed Lazarus." (John 11:41–44, NIV)

Praying for healing often leads up to impatience or frustration toward God. You want what you want, and you want it right now. For those moments, it is easy to slip past the fact that God is God, and His way is not your way!

> As the heavens are higher than the earth, so are my ways higher than your ways and my thoughts than your thoughts. (Isaiah 55:9, NIV)

Whether praying for healing for others or yourself, you need to request that God's will be done. If your request fits into God's will, your request will be answered.

Safety is another subject that comes up in prayer for others or yourself. While the wonders of medication have gone so far up in our years, incredible dangers are still present. Terror attacks, opioid drug addictions, crime, national unrest, cyber attacks, and personal-finance declines still exist. There are a lot of prayers needed.

God also specifies His intentions for prayers being answered.

> When you ask, you do not receive; because you ask with wrong motives, that you may spend what you get on your pleasures. (James 4:3, NIV)

> If you believe, you will receive whatever you ask for in prayer. (Matthew 21:22, NIV)

> Ask and keep on asking and it will be given to you; seek and keep on seeking and you will find; knock and keep on knocking and the door will be opened to you.

> For everyone who keeps on asking receives, and
> he who keeps on seeking finds, and to him who
> keeps on knocking, it will be opened. (Matthew
> 7:7–8, AMP)

Besides the common requests for healing and safety, seek out those extra things that need prayer more often.

More often? More prayers? How does this busy schedule accommodate times for *calling home* to our Father and now adding extra prayers? *Eeek!*

In later chapters, big personal prayers will be covered, but now look at the often overlooked yet desperately needed prayers. Our nation is the most frequently overlooked prayer on my personal prayer list. After all, our nation is a broad, time-consuming subject. Honestly, as of late, the nation is a subject that brings unrest to my soul! However, Christians need to step back and remember who our Father is and what powerful things He can do.

It's hard to mentally fathom that Christians are children of the King. Those children's voices matter! God really values your thoughts and concerns. If your thoughts coincide with His thoughts, He will go above and beyond what you request to answer your prayers.

> Now to Him who is able to do immeasurably
> more than all we ask or imagine, according to
> His power that is at work within us, to Him be
> glory in the church and in Christ Jesus through-
> out all generations, for ever and ever! (Ephesians
> 3:20–21, NIV)

So prayers should be lifted for your nation. God is not a Democrat nor Republican. The picture needs to be processed on a much grander scale. Your nation is your home. The majority wish for families and friends to be able to live peacefully and safely on the streets with children feeling secure to attend school. Most hope for available jobs for hardworking families to support each other. Families from other nations would be welcomed to reside here as long as they are diligently working to improve the economy of the nation and abiding by the rules. If time is offered individually, honestly, and faithfully to lift these topics in prayer, imagine what God can do!

Your community needs your active prayers. Many components make up those communities. Schools, businesses, churches, and recreation centers fill communities with people of every age, race, and gender. Praying for the community doesn't mean just praying for an individual family residing across the street.

There are many homeless children and families in the communities that get overlooked by turning a blind eye. There are teachers who are afraid to teach in their classrooms. There are recreational activities located in the communities, but money may be required to participate. Law enforcement and firefighters put their lives on the line every day. Do those people get lifted individually for prayer, or are they occasionally lifted by a general "please bless our community" prayer?

God isn't asking for an hour just to pray for our firefighters. By taking a moment and being sincere, God will read your hearts. The added advantage is that by praying for individual things in our communities, it creates awareness of your surroundings instead of living with tunnel-vision glasses. A prayer lifted for your community must contain some of the following statements: "Lord, thank You for our police officer and firemen. Please keep them safe in Your arms today. Please flow through our military sons, daughters, fathers, and mothers today. Keep them out of harm's way. Please clear the way so teachers can teach our community's children today. Lord, please help the homeless people today. Let me provide help however I am able. Please light the way for me to help an underprivileged child in a monetary way to be able to participate in activities like sports or music lessons in my community."

Your family needs extra prayers. Family? You may be thinking that you lift prayers for my family a lot. Prayers are indeed lifted when they're sick, for safety, family drama, thanksgiving, and praise for accomplishments. What else is there to pray for?

Faith walk. Today.

Whether or not your children are two years old or sixty years old, every day they face the challenges of a very sinful world. Each experiences the wiles and torments of Satan. Each child is faced with the temptations of the day, whether it be running with dangerous friends, alcohol, disobeying an authority figure, utilizing extra supplies secretly from an office, lying to a friend, or hiding a fast-food receipt.

Do you lift prayers every day requesting God's shield for them while facing those temptations? I am ashamed to say, I do not. Do you lift prayers daily requesting for them to see God's light clearly and live their lives as one of God's beacons of hope? I am ashamed to say, I do not. Do you lift prayers daily requesting helpful ways to encourage them to be good stewards of what God has provided? I am ashamed to say, I do not. Do you lift prayers daily that they will accomplish great things for God during their short time here on earth? I am ashamed to say, I do not. Do you lift prayers that your character will mirror God's love and concern for them? I am ashamed to say, I do not. (I might mirror that God forgives over and over again for the bad choices I make so often.)

These spiritual faith-walk prayers need to be lifted to God often. These prayers can be intersection-stoplight prayers. These are not questions that you are trying to solve. These are prayers that are lifted up to God to accomplish.

Take this challenge. Pray one of these prayers for your family. The next time you stop at an intersection (pray with eyes open, of course!), be mindful that Satan will try to block your prayer or distract you from praying. Your phone will ring, you'll receive a text message, or a favorite song will come on the radio. But don't be distracted or discouraged. Just smile and realize that it must be important for Satan to be interested at all!

Families in various walks of their lives represent the needed prayer within the different communities. The lost, the wrong-turn, scenic-route, noncar owners represent of an assortment of neighbors in the community. Family members, neighbors, fellow employees— all fall under these categories.

Once again, this is the time for clamoring for methods or road signs. Lifting these people up to God shows the awareness of these needs. God will grant clarity and interactions if it is in His will.

The *lost* are people who have gotten caught up in bad patterns. They may have started out in Christian families or environments, but now they exist in a place where Christian ways are far off in the distance. Addictions, resentment, anger at God or the church, new surroundings, big roadblocks into their return to a relationship with Jesus—they feel like there is no possible way for them to return (at least not today), and for these moments, they really don't care!

A prayer for the lost could be as follows: "Lord, I pray that You lift up ———. Please knock down the barrier that is controlling them right now. Flow through their addiction, anger, and fears with Your Spirit so they can get the help they need. Please surround them with people who can shine Your light on the path to get back. In Jesus's name, Amen."

Wrong-turn Christians have made wrong choices that make them feel like they are not acceptable church people. The sin they have committed causes them to feel unwelcomed, uncomfortable, or embarrassed. Sometimes they miss fellowship with believers, but they can't seem to find the right time or road to return. A prayer for wrong-turn Christians could be as follows: "Lord, there is no sin that is too big for You. Thank You for Your loving forgiveness. Please remove all negative thoughts and fear that follows remorse. Please keep reassuring sinners that it's never too late to return. In Jesus's name, amen."

Scenic-route Christians are those who readily admit that they are Christians and belong to a church. Life gets in the way, and they don't get to attend as often as they probably should. These are the families that always adamantly attend on Easter and Christmas. However, their Sundays get filled with sports' commitments, mowing, laundry, social activities, activities of leisure such as shopping, golf, or swimming at the pool.

Scenic-route Christians probably get overlooked most of all because they meld right in. The evangelistic Christians are trying to reach out and engage people outside of the faith. The scenic-route Christians are good, upstanding citizens who attend church. So why would they need your prayers? Hmmm.

Prayer for scenic-route Christians could be lifted as follows: "Lord, please open all ears, eyes, hearts to be able to clearly see that worshipping You is the first priority. All the busyness and activities will disappear, but You will last forever. Help all to see the riches that You unfold from heaven for those who show obedience. In Jesus's name, Amen."

No-car folks need more consistent and heartfelt prayers for their survival and the missionaries who are trying to reach out to them. No-car folks can't be classified as lost, wrong-turn, or scenic drivers because they don't have a car in the first place! Many live in violent and scary places where Christianity is banned. They don't know the truths about God.

They don't know that God is a loving and all-powerful King who can rescue them from any poverty and destruction. They don't know that this imperfect and painful life is very short compared to the paradise that God promises to those who believe. It's impossible for the no-car folks to believe something that they haven't heard. That's where God's missionaries come in.

> So neither the one who plants nor the one who waters is anything, but only God, who makes things grow. The one who plants and the one who waters have one purpose, and they will each be rewarded according to their own labor. For we are co-workers in God's service; you are God's field, God's building. (1 Corinthians: 3:7–8, NIV)

The missionaries or planters who are trying to follow God's directive are in grave danger many times as much as the no-car folks.

> Therefore go and make disciples of all nations, baptizing them in the name of the Father and of the Son and of the Holy Spirit. (Matthew 28:19, NIV)

Missionaries and their families in third-world countries are in danger of violence, disease, and disobedience to other governments. The nation where you reside also has missionaries in danger. Violence is rampant on the streets, and no one is safe, especially targeted Christians. They get lumped in with enemy competitive gangs as people who need to stay away from the territory.

A prayer for the no-car folks could be lifted as follows: "Lord, please help the missionaries, near and far, to have safe opportunities to share Your gospel of Jesus Christ with those who need to hear it. Open ears, eyes, and hearts to those listening. Let Your Word be planted to them to prosper and grow. In Jesus's name, Amen."

The list of others that need our prayers is immense. God tells us to ask, and we are asking!

Somehow, when praying for others, two things happen. It is realized when the focus is on the lives of others that your own life may not seem as drastic in comparison. The problems or challenges that you may be facing don't compare with the outcomes, horrors, or devastations that others are living with. A better perspective is gained on how blessed your life truly is!

The second thing that happens while focusing on others is that self-problems or needs are not emphasized. There is no time to wallow!

CHAPTER 22

YIELD SIGN

Yielding is the last ingredient needed for our scratch recipe for prayer. This ingredient is the most needed for prayer, yet most distasteful ingredient for many bakers. Yielding, a very course, difficult ingredient while mixing, takes time and effort to get the right consistency. Yielding is probably right next to *repenting* under levels of difficulty in the prayer module.

An often-substituted name coinciding with the ingredient of yielding is *change*. Change is the dirty word that most don't care for. For many, an unpleasant but familiar situation is more palatable than to walk into unfamiliar territory.

Christians have to make a conscious effort to yield in many cases because it does not come naturally to any.

You probably have no problems as a Christian *praising* God for the wonderful blessings in your life. Many times, you may genuinely feel remorse, asking for forgiveness. Requests made to God come naturally, and you don't have any second thoughts making them. But yielding? That is a whole different story.

> You need to persevere so that when you have done the will of God, you will receive what he has promised. (Hebrews 10:36, NIV)

The Ten Commandments were rules that Christians were given to hinder sinning. Most understand about yielding to God's will of not breaking His rules (at least we *attempt* to follow the rules!).

However, there are areas that are often casually overlooked when thinking of *yielding*. Traveling down this overgrown brush will be attempted in the chapter ahead.

Three hundred and sixty-five times in the Bible, God says not to be afraid. (Three hundred and sixty-five times! Isn't that a coincidence? Or a God incidence!)

> Peace I leave with you; my peace I give you. I do not give to you as the world gives. Do not let your hearts be troubled and do not be afraid. (John 14:27, NIV)

Yielding to God is usually associated with God calling missionaries to do His work in dangerous places. Obviously, that is a request for God's will that surely brings fear. Yielding to fear and safety is never an easy decision. Missionaries, like the disciples, accomplish amazing work for God. The baseball coach in the movie *A Field of Dreams* says, "Of course, it's not easy, or everyone would do it." Yielding to God's will where safety is questioned, of course, is not easy. There are truly faithful servants who have the level of faith to answer this call.

Yielding to God's instruction over fear of bodily harm appears various times in the Bible. Ananias was given the marching nudge from God to visit Saul when he was hunting and jailing and killing Christians. Ananias reminded God of this fact, but God sent him anyway. Yielding by Ananias led to Saul becoming a Christian, changing his name to Paul and becoming the all-time face on the front page of who's who in the Christian world. Ananias is indeed a role model for Faith 101!

Nehemiah was another example of a man who yielded to God's command. He was a Jew living in an area, which is now named Iran or Persia. Having worked himself up through the ranks, he served at the palace as the king of Persia's cherished cupbearer. Nehemiah asked some Jewish friends how his fellow Jews were doing in Jerusalem. They informed him that the people were living in disgrace. The walls were knocked down, and Jerusalem's gates had been burned. Nehemiah was mortified. He prayed to God for the next four months concerning His will. God's will for Nehemiah was to leave the comforts of the palace and return to Jerusalem to rebuild the wall. Talk about yielding!

The first step toward a solution for dealing with fears of yielding is brutal honesty with God. He already knows you inside and out. He will gladly grant assistance and clarity if you ask Him for help.

Christians are famous for covering up fears. Making excuses such as lack of enjoyment or busyness dismisses God's directive. Underneath the excuses lies fear.

God will grant all the needed help when yielding to His desires. He knows all weaknesses and fears. If fear and anxiety are placed at God's feet with willingness to yield, there will be success. God will bring His will into fruition.

Yielding to God may be a change using subtraction rather than addition. Yes, there are aspects of your personality that God would like you to yield to Him and dispose of. (Of course, He would not change a thing about my "perfectness" and wonderful disposition!)

My dear Pastor Bob used to say that when you are facing a challenge or discrepancy with others, step back and contemplate what role you played in the issue. Confrontations will occasionally occur with others from time to time. Headstrong, overly self-confident, impulsive (without planning ahead), emotional, hotheaded, and volatile personality traits will inevitably lead to conflicts. When finding yourself in a conflict, consciously make the effort to step back and contemplate what role you played in this conflict.

A familiar trait in our personality that's often hard to yield is pride. Yielding pride is very important to God because there are numerous verses that He points to saying that lives are not all about oneself: yielding and submitting mean great rewards in heaven!

Two disciples found themselves resisting God's command by requesting something from Jesus.

> Then James and John, the sons of Zebedee, came
> to him. "Teacher," they said, "we want you to do
> for us whatever we ask."

"What do you want me to do for you?" he asked.

They replied, "Let one of us sit at your right and the other at your left in your glory."

"You don't know what you are asking," Jesus said. "Can you drink the cup I drink or be baptized with the baptism I am baptized with?"

"We can," they answered.

Jesus said to them, "You will drink the cup I drink and be baptized with the baptism I am baptized with, but to sit at my right or left is not for me to grant. These places belong to those for whom they have been prepared." (Mark 10:35–41, NIV)

Feeling like special treatment is deserved occurs frequently. *Entitlement* is worn on the shirtsleeves. God is very clear that He sees things differently. Get down and dirty and become servants to others. Make the decision to overlook the drama when the feeling appears that someone is receiving the attention that should be directed at you. Remember, God is prepared to award one yielding their pride.

So the last will be first, and the first will be last. (Matthew 20:16, NIV)

In the end, regardless of how much Christian servanthood is sacrificed for church, each person is just as ridden with sin as the next guy. We are not entitled to any special gift from God—end of story. God has graciously chosen us, not because of any sacrifice that we have made.

The gift is free.

CHAPTER 23

REMBRANDT

Why would the most prestigious, most glorified King in the world want to take time to listen?

> Or do you not know that your body is a temple of the Holy Spirit within you, whom you have from God? You are not your own, for you were bought with a price. So glorify God in your body. (1 Corinthians 6:19–20, NIV)

God created you. You are His precious handiwork—His masterpiece. The familiar story of creation has been replayed many times since childhood. When reading something for the millionth time, sometimes God sheds a new light, and the story is seen in a different way. Christians are God's masterpieces. A lot of thought, time and talent was poured into His creation. God created each differently, yet all the same.

Farshad Asl, entrepreneur, states, "What makes you different is what makes you stronger. You are a masterpiece uniquely designed by God. You can have tremendous victories, love, and abundance." Robert A. Heinlein, American novelist, states the obvious:

> Anybody can look at a pretty girl and see a pretty girl. An artist can look at a pretty girl and see the old woman she will become. A better artist can look at an old woman and see the pretty girl that

she used to be. But a great artist—a master—and that is what Auguste Rodin was--can look at an old woman, portray her exactly as she is... and force the viewer to see the pretty girl she used to be... and more than that, he can make anyone with the sensitivity of an armadillo, or even you, see that this lovely young girl is still alive, not old and ugly at all, but simply prisoned inside her ruined body.

God is that artist. He creates someone beautiful and foresees the beautiful old woman she will become. When she becomes aged, He still sees the beautiful person that she used to be. God brings the young girl to the surface, no matter what outer covering is there. She is not ugly or old, just simply prisoned inside her ruined body. Because of the masterful artist that He is, He will release her from that tattered body and free her to be young and beautiful forever. That's the artist who created masterpiece after masterpiece.

Richard McKinley, world-renowned landscape artist, offers advice to artists about how to create a masterpiece. He starts his guidance with encouragement to employ the three Ws: why, what, and when. If you know the *why*, the emotional connection to a subject/scene, it can answer the *what*. The what is what needs to be added and what to leave out, ultimately creating an air of mystery that engages the viewer. The what leads to the *when*. When is a painting finished? The painting is done when the main purpose/concept behind the painting is achieved. It is a full circle.

Why did God create you? God created you with a love so great that He let His cherished Son die to save you. The purpose of your whole existence is to bring glory and honor to Him. He created you to love what He loves and to appreciate the beauty around you that He created.

Special characteristics were formed into the masterpieces that He created. Unique gifts and talents that no one else shares are found in His creations. God rises above mastering a doctorate degree in design, biology, chemistry, and anatomy, to only mention a few. Some amazing facts about the body are as follows:

- Lungs breathe 74 quarts of air per minute while exercising.
- Hearts pump 200 gallons of blood per day.
- There are 600 muscles that move to help organs work together.
- The heart beats 100,000 times per day and sends blood from one end to other in less than one minute.
- Lungs deliver air through 1,500 miles of airways.
- The brain has 100 billion nerve cells and signals 200 miles per hour.
- The body is estimated to have 60,000 miles of blood vessels.
- Blood vessels, end to end, would wrap more than 2 times around earth.
- The liver has over 500 functions.
- Sneezes travel 100 mph, and coughs travel 60 mph.
- Saliva over a lifetime would fill 2 swimming pools.
- Noses can remember 50,000 different scents.
- The body uses 200 muscles to take one step, and frowns use 43 muscles.
- The body gives off enough heat in 30 minutes to bring ½ gal of water to a boil.

> For we are God's handiwork, created in Christ
> Jesus to do good works, which God prepared in
> advance for us to do. (Ephesians 2:10, NIV)

You were created as a masterpiece. Every time you hear that negative voice from Satan reminding you of how worthless you are, turn your thoughts back to creation. God created you as His masterpiece. He has amazingly fine-tuned plans for your future.

> "For I know the plans I have for you," declares the
> Lord, "plans to prosper you and not to harm you,

plans to give you hope and a future." (Jeremiah 29:11, NIV)

God's masterpiece is a beautiful quilt that is made up of many exquisite and unique patterns. His plan for your life is intertwined with many other lives. Your individual, personal life makes up your own quilt square, but your square fits snuggly next to others.

Together, with all of the unique characteristics, a beautiful masterpiece is created. That masterpiece could be a connection of many different groups: families, churches, schools, teams, and work places.

American quilts were created for various purposes; warmth, decoration, and even to represent important heritage. Like quilts, a person's life has many different purposes.

One's purpose to family could indeed be all of the above: warmth, comfort, and decoration. It is important to make family members feel beautiful and appreciated. Also, if the baton is not handed off to the next generation, important historical facts will be lost. Relaying a family's or church's heritage shows the challenges, will and commitment that forefathers went through to get your family to the place where it thrives today.

The make-up of churches is very similar. Attractive quilts are beautiful to behold. These quilts can be bright and colorful with squares making exquisite patterns. Like this type of quilt, some churches are big, and stylish. The members are uniform and add to the grandeur.

Some churches are traditional and formal. In order to belong, one must have similar qualities in their quilt squares as the group.

Some quilts are a hodge- podge combination of many different squares that come together to make one quilt.

There is a wonderful contemporary song called "City on the Hill" by a Christian band called Casting Crowns. The song talks about how important the different people are in a church. Some are soldiers, poets, young, old, dancers and they need each other for the church to thrive and survive.

Each working square fits into God's masterpiece of all masterpieces. God's desire is for your unique square to fit snuggly and harmoniously into the working squares that surround you. The ties that bind you are the weavings of your faith and purpose that God has masterfully woven for your life.

CHAPTER 24

THE "SELFIE" OF DESTRUCTION

Most Christians are purposeful about avoiding hurting others, yet sin against self occurs many times. The jags vary between clearly visible tears to choices of putting yourself down for the sake of others. The body is a temple of God. So how and why are bodies mistreated? What happens to the dreams of a peaceful life that are being replaced with abuse?

> For to set the mind on the flesh is death, but
> to set the mind on the Spirit is life and peace.
> (Romans 8:6-NIV)

Addiction is a deadly way that bodies are mistreated. It festers as a compulsion, dependence, or an obsession that one day survival without is virtually impossible. Every thought surrounds this compulsion. Every decision is an avenue to help this controlling addiction to continue comfortably existing. The dependence takes over all reasoning: including what's right, wrong, legal, honorable, and trustworthy.

Reasoning could include escaping from emotional pain, emotional illnesses such as depression and anxiety, stress, and childhood drama that went unresolved. Alcoholics, drug addicts, and sex addicts are not searching for *feeling good* but *feeling less*. Addiction is probably the most frequent answer for ways to mistreat our bodies. But not all addictions are blatant and loud like alcohol or drugs.

Addiction to work is quiet and socially acceptable. This controlling addiction is often overlooked and even admired by others. The only people who know that they are swayed by these compulsions are families or addicts themselves. Others realize that this person is driven and invested, and do not view the work as a compulsion.

The spectrum of success in the corporate world corresponds to the employee hours put in. Workdays are not based on the needs of families or responsibilities outside of the workplace. Business locations are not centered on the well-being of employees. Many businessmen and women fly all over the country or even the world for meetings and business happenings. The corporate world looks at success in this way: people are acknowledged for the high pace and commitment of getting an end goal to completion. From the outside, these work addicts are viewed as successful, well-dressed, and put-together employees. Only they can feel the inner pull of addiction that controls the actions in their lives.

Some Christians work in a more stationary office or in the home as a parent rather than working in that corporate frenzy. The question to ask is the following: when waking up in the morning, do you hit the floor running with a to-do list, realizing that you are already falling behind before getting started? This frame of mind is an addiction that damages God's temples as well. The list does not get set aside until the following day after the second or third cup of coffee!

Submitting to the false god of food is also a silent addiction. Every chosen social interaction somehow has food related to it: family get-togethers, having lunch with a distraught friend, snacks at work, baking frenzies, and cooking shows. The list is endless.

What happens when a neighbor has encountered a tragedy? A cake is baked. How are teachers thanked for hard work and dedication? Delicious chocolate chip cookies are baked. Food is served on an emotional level beyond necessary means of eating to survive.

Addictions of any kind cause pain to the temple that God created.

Negative words are another way of causing harm. Attempts may be made to refrain from hurting others. Parents remind children that if having nothing nice to say, not to say anything, anything at all. Words to others can really cut like a knife, yet the words that you allow yourself to think are just as dangerous. How many times, when trying to plan or accomplish something, does a cutting voice in your head saying the following: "It's not going to turn out. Why did you even start this? No one will appreciate it anyway. No one pays attention to all the work you put in."

You probably are your own worst enemy in this regard, never criticizing or holding such high standards at this level to another person. Those cutting thoughts targeted at yourself cut you down before even getting started!

God created people as puzzle pieces. He did not throw all the parts together in a haphazard way. Everyone is part of a grand picture. The pieces fit snuggly into the other puzzle pieces. God knows ahead of time about the strength is needed to get something accomplished. He knows what the challenges will be. That is why He created you the way He did and placed you in the very time slot of your life. He knows your needs for fitting snuggly into those lives around you.

> He will make your innocence radiate like the dawn, and the justice of your cause will shine like the noonday sun. The justice of our cause like the noonday sun! (Psalm 37:5, NLV)

Why then do you second-guess the skills or abilities needed to accomplish His work?

The question to start with when you begin hearing those negative jabs is, for what reason are you trying to accomplish this? Is this act an ingredient needed while following God's will? Ask Him for clarification. Many times, God's will is gauged on your own perceptions. God's will encompasses big things, right? Religious movements, programs, seminars, studies, and evangelism techniques? How could God's will include putting a luncheon together or handing bulletins out at a service? Again, ask God for clarification.

The second thing needed when feeling stressed about a service is to stop looking at weaknesses and fears for five minutes. Look at the *you* that God so lovingly created. Big or small, what things are you good at? Take the time and thank God for your puzzle piece in the grand picture of life and the time slot that He placed you in. "God, I don't know what the big picture is. Thank You for making me the hot mess that I am. Please use me to be Your vessel to help get Your work accomplished. Amen."

He will bring His will to fruition, providing all the needed elements to make it happen.

The third component needed after saying a prayer for clarification is to stop, look, and listen. Parents teach children how to safely cross a street. Christians need to follow the same steps before planning some event in service to God. God provides all the essentials needed to accomplish an event within His will. Many times, stress comes from feeling overwhelmed because attempts are made to accomplish too many things alone. Desires to avoid bothering someone or becoming too needy add on stress and anxiety. Piles and piles of services are heaped onto one's own to-do list. Not one thing excels because too many things are happening that one person is trying to solely accomplish.

Rely on others to follow the same routine of asking God to clarify His will. If a person denies your request for assisting on a task, ask another person. Don't take it personally. That person may not be a fit for this particular event. Some other time, they might be willing and able to help out. On the flip side, don't get involved in an event for God just because you are asked. Truly ask God for clarification. If the answer is yes, give it your all. If the answer is no, tell the person who is asking, at this time, you can't help, but please continue asking in the future.

You need to perceive the picture of yourself the same way that God views you. You are fearfully and wonderfully made. The purpose of your life is to be God's vessel, serving Him for the short time that you are here. In your prayer life, as you pray for Jesus, others, and yourself, offer up to God the person that He created—you!

Erase the negative attacks on yourself by surrounding yourself with the promises that God has laid in front of you. Fill yourself with these promises. You will feel the power that Jesus created you to have in His name.

CHAPTER 25

GOD'S SYMPHONY

By now, you realize that indeed you were born with a purpose in mind. You are not whimsically sent to be alive on this earth for no reason. You play an important role in God's orchestra.

A book titled *Just David* impacted the way God's symphony is viewed. After reading it multiple times, my view on life in general is enhanced greatly. The story is about a young boy who was being raised by his father isolated from people. They both play the violin. David is raised to *play* sunsets, his lake, trees, nature, etc. The father is becoming increasingly ill, so he tries to return David to civilization. The father dies in a barn before they make it. The only things found on him are a couple scraps of paper with an indiscernible signature.

David nor the family that raised him realized that the father was a famous violinist who disappeared from civilization with his son six years before his death. David was raised not knowing about evil or sadness or money. He was raised to look at the beauty around him and play beautiful music. One of the important lessons that David's father taught him was that he was one little instrument in the great orchestra of life. David must always play his masterpiece in tune and must never drag or be a discord.

God's orchestra is the same. He has created distinctive gifts within Christians to play important parts in His symphony. The church body is His orchestra. He is the conductor. Your instrument helps to create a wonderful song. But, if you drag or are a discord, it's noticeable. Christians all play special and different instruments in God's orchestra.

An orchestra is made up of *string, woodwind, brass,* and *percussion* instruments. The string instruments, hollow inside to allow sound to vibrate within them, are made of different kinds of wood, but the part of the instrument that makes the sound is the strings, which are made of nylon, steel, or sometimes gut. The strings are played most often by drawing a *bow* across them. The handle of the bow is made of wood, and the strings of the bow are actually horsehair from horses' tails! Sometimes the musicians will use their fingers to pluck the strings, and occasionally they will turn the bow upside down and play the strings with the wooden handle.

Although fewer instruments to choose from, the strings have the most instruments in the orchestra: the violin, viola, cello, and the large double bass. The smaller instruments, the violin and viola, make higher-pitched sounds while the larger cello and double bass produce low rich sounds. Each instrument is needed in the melody.

A preschool prayer resonates this fact about God's orchestra: "Some people are big, some people are small. It doesn't matter because God loves us all." The British poet Samuel Butler's essay "How to Make the Best of Life" contains a line that states that life is like playing a violin in public and learning the instrument as one goes on. Sometimes while playing a solo, a violinist makes mistakes, stumbles, trips, and falls. Then comes the embarrassment.

Those playing the string instrument roles in God's orchestra must take chances, make mistakes, stumble, and fall and try again.

Play God's instrument at your church. Step out of the comfort zone and take chances. Don't wait until your song is without any flaws because that will never happen. Take that step doing all that you can do and do it to His glory and honor. Your life will never be the same!

Woodwind instruments, part of the wind family, include many popular instruments such as the flute, piccolo, clarinet, saxophone and oboes, bassoons, English horns. Most woodwind instruments share a similar key system which allows players to more easily move between woodwind instruments as compared to brass instruments. It is common for a saxophone player to be able to play flute or clarinet with a small amount of practice since the fingering systems are so similar.

Who are woodwind players at your church? These are the people who have mastered a skill from the outside world and are eagerly able to use that talent in a different venue, giving back within the church. A good friend, a brick mason by trade, created a beautiful brick cross in the courtyard walkway. Perhaps a roofer can use talents to work on roof at church, or an electrician utilizes skills to install a new welcoming sign.

Shawls are lovingly croqueted or knitted and given to those who are suffering through prayer shawl ministries. (A previous chapter made you aware that I am not a woodwind instrument in God's symphony, using my sewing ability for any Christian purpose!)

Brass instruments in an orchestra have a distinctive sound and can play louder than any other in the orchestra. Who are brass members in my church? Usually, this person wears many different hats depending on what is asked of them at the time. These people do not haphazardly take on a special job without a history, knowledge, and practice. Not afraid for their voices to be heard, they show pride and conviction for their work.

Percussion instruments are those instruments where a sound comes from striking or scraping the instrument. Generally, percussion instruments are the background instruments whose purpose is to maintain the rhythm and support the other instruments. Timpanis, xylophones, cymbals, triangles, snare drums, tambourines, bass drums, maracas, gongs, chimes are percussion instruments that might be heard in a symphony.

The percussionists at a church might be the altar guild who makes sure God's sacrament is available and ready to be used to divinely bless by pastors. These treasured servants serve behind the scenes and know the traditions, history, and colors of the altar linens. The holy altar is always adorned with beautiful flowers, especially on special holidays, and much care is put into its arrangement.

This altar percussionist always keeps the rhythm and adds color and excitement. The focus is rarely centered on them, but their meaningful jobs support other members in the bigger picture. They are comfortable supporting and not playing solos.

Worship time is God's "opus," playing in the realm of heaven. The definition of an *opus* is "a separate composition or set of compositions by a particular composer." God is the composer! He created you to be the special instruments coming together with the other created instruments of the great symphony to bring glory, honor, and thanksgiving to God. Look within and ask some important questions to the person inside looking out. Do you truly view yourself as an indispensable instrument in God's great symphony? What family of instruments do you see yourself falling under? Are you performing your very best and contributing your gifts to the song being played? Do your notes ever cause discord or drag?

Christians are never perfect. Some days (many days!) the notes may drag, and the song falls well below what is possible! Some days are filled with discords around every corner. God knows you. God know me. He never stops offering His grace, mercy, and forgiveness. He is always awaiting the majestic sounds of His orchestra. God knows and hears each of His instruments. He created some to be woodwind, brass, and some to be percussion. All shapes, styles, appearances, and tones are different.

God is the director of each note. He never tires of telling His musicians when to come in, hold back, and when to stop! The ability to play perfectly in-tune music in God's orchestra appears only when you stop focusing solely on the sounds of your own instrument. By doing this, you can listen for His commands and hear His guidance!

CHAPTER 26

PEOPLE ARE CREATED DIFFERENTLY

C reating a more peaceful life and fulfilling faith walk is completely possible by making some adjustments in perceptions of what is around you. Accept and utilize differences in yourself and others to improve your quality of life. Simple solution, right?

My husband and I once attended a Family Life Marriage Conference for alumni (having gone once before, so now we were "alumni"). The seminar was called "Understanding One Another." The instructor gave us a DISC Relationship Profile questionnaire with answers as "most" or "least" After finishing the questionnaire and tallying the answers, the instructions were to go to one of four different groups based on the answers collected.

The instruction was for one person to be the spokesperson for their group after discussion. As a reader, you are entitled to be a fly on the wall. Dominance Group was loudly arguing over who should be the spokesperson. Influencing/Fun Group was laughing loudly and making jokes. Keep-Peace Group was filled with people shaking their heads and shuddering at acting as the spokesperson. And the Conscientious/ Make-It-Right Group was quietly talking about who had the most essential experiences to act as the spokesperson.

God created each person to have different personality types. Whether in a church, workplace, associations with friends or family members in our homes, the dominant parts of personalities will surface. The choice is yours: You can try to dominate above someone else's personality, or you can utilize those strengths to help improve your quality of living. In every encounter, a dominant person should not make all the decisions, for there are some issues where other personality types need to fight for their beliefs.

But for everyday, trivial issues, remember that other person's strengths. People are wired very differently. God created every person with strength within. If these strengths are utilized in everyday lives and people stop trying to insert their own type of strengths on others, everyone's lives would be much more peaceful. Work would be more productive because each person would act in ways that fit the strongpoints of their personality.

An amazing program called Iditarod Teacher on the Trail permits educators to spend a week in Alaska, bringing the experiences to their classrooms and making education come alive. The ages of learners don't matter; each concept can be adapted into any age lesson.

What is the Iditarod? The Iditarod Trail Sled Dog Race is an annual long-distance dog-sled race run in early March, lasting approximately nine to fifteen days. It takes place entirely in the state of Alaska. Mushers start with a team of twenty-one dogs. Teams generally race through blizzards causing whiteout conditions, subzero temperatures, and gale-force winds. The windchill can reach −100 °F. The trail runs into the sparsely populated inner Alaska, and then along the shore of the Bering Sea, finally reaching Nome in Western Alaska. The trail is through harsh tundra and forests, over hills and mountain passes, and across rivers, through widely separated towns and villages, settlements.

Environments in churches can grow and improve in the same ways that Iditarod Teachers on the Trail were trying to improve classrooms. If church environments improve one step at a time, as an individual, your own life would improve, one surface at a time.

Pastors should be like the dog mushers. The musher guides his team with "Gee!" which is the command for a right turn, and "Haw!" the command for a left turn. "Whoa" means "slow down and come to a halt." The pacing of the dogs is watched carefully by the musher to ensure the team moves along the trail safely. The pastor is the leader, commander. He should be trusted and his commands followed.

There are times on the Iditarod trail where there may be several paths to take. How do the dogs know where to go? When a dog team is well trained, they listen and follow the correct command from their musher to guide them the correct way so they won't make a wrong turn. Teamwork is essential at its best.

You need to listen and follow your pastor's commands. If half of the dog team pulled one direction and the other half pulled the other direction, not only would the team not be safe, but they wouldn't get anywhere toward the destination. A pastor's leadership is crucial and essential for your race through life. The pastor also tells his parishioners, "Whoa," when they need to slow down or stop in some detrimental actions of life that perhaps parishioners are participating in.

Martin Buser was a four-time Iditarod winner. In 2014, early on in the race, he obtained injuries that prevented him from being the strong musher that he had always been. He had to count on the dogs to help him finish the race. Buser still finished in sixth place after the harrowing experience. He had to lean on the characteristics of his dogs.

Martin Buser says that a good sled dog is like a good person: hardworking, honest, friendly with a positive attitude, curious, with a heart and willingness and desire to get the job accomplished. These are the needed characteristics of our fellow workers.

One of the things that Teachers on the Trail do when traveling to Alaska to learn creative education strategies is talk to the dog mashers about their techniques about leadership and environment. These teachers combine field knowledge with educator's knowledge to create a wonderful learning classroom environment.

An important educators' fact is that humans retain information with three very different learning styles. *Visual-style learners* gain the most knowledge from reading and watching. *Auditory-style learners* thrive while listening and discussing. *Kinesthetic-style learners* are active, hands-on learners. Life is the largest classroom for learning and storing amazing information. How can one examine the facts in the world and still not believe in God?

Life's textbook, the Bible, shares the information about what your time should be spent thinking about.

> Finally, brothers and sisters, whatever is true, whatever is noble, whatever is right, whatever is pure, whatever is lovely, whatever is admirable— if anything is excellent or praiseworthy—think about such things. (Philippians 4:8, NIV)

If more learning is spent in fun and exciting ways, there wouldn't be much time for all the bickering and stress. You have so few free moments as it is. If minds were filled with praiseworthy things, days would be filled with wonder and excitement—one surface and one thought at a time. How can the creative-learning /Iditarod characteristics be applied to the homelife and churches to create a great learning environment?

Visual learners like to read and watch. We have an ongoing joke in our family about cooking. When trying a new recipe, directions are carefully read and followed. The most favored scenario is to carefully watch someone make this recipe and try to follow along. My husband and daughter are kinesthetic learners or *recipe dumpers*, as I call them. They don't measure. Recipes merely provide temperatures and signs that point them toward the direction that they want to go. Over time, our family has learned to laugh about this and not judge the others for their techniques.

Creative-learning approach works in churches of all denominations also. Members have very different learning styles. Knowledgeable pastors who want to teach parishioners some biblical knowledge approach them in ways like a great teacher. Different learning styles are incorporated into the message so each person can gain the maximum insight.

For a specific topic, the visual learners need to read or write. Some pastors have parishioners use a Bible during sermons to look up verses. As they find the verse for themselves, the pastor reads the verse with them. Some ministers also encourage members to take notes during the sermon. However, just like the recipe "dumpers" do not judge others for their learning styles or try to enforce your learning style on them. If you are not a visual learner, it's not mandatory that sermon notes be taken! By doing this, visual learners are reached by reading and taking notes, auditory learners by hearing his sermon, and kinesthetic learners by allowing and encouraging them to "do something active" during his sermon.

The sermons are not the only way to connect with people in worship. Music is an integral part of worship in every denomination. In more contemporary services, members could be given small musical tambourines to actively participate. Instead, be filled with the Spirit, speaking to one another with psalms, hymns, and songs from the Spirit. Sing and make music from your heart to the Lord, (Ephesians 5:18,19, NIV) In traditional services, even old hymns can incorporate some actions for worship. Actions don't have to be loud clapping and wild hand-raising or clapping. "How Great Thou Art" for kinesthetic learners could be as the following:

O Lord my God,
When I in awesome wonder *(hands on cheeks)*
Consider all the worlds
Thy Hands have made *(folded hands)*
I see the stars *(finger pointing up)*
I hear the roaring thunder *(finger on ear)*
Thy power throughout the universe displayed
(finger pointing up)

Then sings my soul *(hand on heart)*
My Savior God, to Thee *(folded hands)*
How great Thou art
How great Thou art
Then sings my soul
My Savior God, to Thee
How great Thou art
How great Thou art!

In order to thrive, each Christian has to feel accepted and not judged for his or her learning style. So if you want to quietly do actions representing the song, do it. If you are not the kinesthetic type, don't do it. But don't feel pressured either way.

God has a plan for our lives (yes, I think this totals one hundred times that you have heard about this plan through this book). All people are born with different personalities, appearances, skills, backgrounds. Some are leaders, followers, servers musical, hands-on, solitary, mechanical, vocal, rough-around-the-edges and articulate.

How would you describe yourself? What part do you think God wants you to play in His symphony, the church? Ask Him. He will graciously lead you there.

CHAPTER 27

REASON FOR THE SEASON

I s anyone out there? Am I all alone? I feel like I can't cope with anything. I've been praying and praying. I don't see any sign that anyone is listening. God promised to lead me, and I don't think He is here at all. Do any of these questions sound familiar?

Cancer, heart attack, death of a child, depression, fire, budgets, hurricane, divorce, injury, being laid off—all these words bring peaceful lives to a dark, scary, treacherous time. You just want to get off this ride! Not a short time later, not tomorrow, *right now.* I am a good and faithful person. So where is God in all of this? I've prayed over and over. Why hasn't God come to move this mountain of anguish? Where are You, God? You made a promise!

> If you believe, you will receive whatever you ask
> for in prayer. (Matthew 21:22, NIV)

If you believe? I don't understand! *I believe!* Sound familiar?

How many times do you pray for something, thinking that this is the preferred answer to be, but it's not truly possible. The doctors say there's no cure, the miserable job will never change, and the abuse will never stop, yada, yada, yada.

Unfortunately, the most notable times when your faith life is strengthened are the times of hardship. During hardships is when you are at your weakest points. Your body feels beyond tired—to the bone. You cry, feel angry, question, and doubt. You want to throw in the towel, give up, and be done. Your faith feels as battered as your mind and body. Your life seems hopeless. Any strength that you possessed before now has just evaporated and disappeared.

This is when your faith is tested and strengthened. It is only after you reach the top of the worst crest that you begin to see a newly strengthened faith peeking through.

Don't misunderstand. This amazing moment does not, in any way, quell your grief or frustration. These moments of clarity only allow the light of happy things to flicker in the darkness.

Hardships in your life can come in physical as well as emotional ways. The human body has a way of telling you when something is wrong. Weeks may pass, turning the warning sounds down to a minimal volume. You plod on despite the signs. Then the hammer comes crashing down, and you hear the voice of a surgeon saying that you have to undergo surgery. Some days feel like the very rug under your feet is being ripped out. The test results come back showing some debilitating disease, like cancer.

During an extreme illness, all parts of your body feel this paralyzing hardship. Not only are you covered with pain, discomfort, and weakness, but fear also sets in. Not only is death itself feared, but fears of inability to provide future care for family members washes through. You feel like you are drowning and too weak to even tread water.

A friend lost her husband unexpectedly and had to pull strength from the bottom of her soul to continue on with life for her children. God helped her to draw strength from places like sports games, holidays, graduations, which first appeared to be quicksand.

Christians are taught at an early age to believe what cannot be seen: "For we live by faith, not by sight" (2 Corinthians 5:7, NIV). That's easily said when you are thanking God for all the joy in your life: birth of a child, weddings, promotions at work, and sunny vacations. But how do you navigate through hard times when you see no reasoning or understanding?

Try to put yourselves on autopilot through the storms of life. When times are rocky, with the storm raging, lean on God's promise that He is the pilot. Looking for landmarks is impossible. Sudden turbulence and jolts shake you. You can't see out of the window because the sky is black and foreboding. Lean on God's promises that He will never leave you. He will bring us through this storm.

How do airline pilots navigate where they are going? Long ago, pilots had to navigate by looking out the window. They counted on visual landmarks or stars in the sky. In the 1920s, the earliest airmail carriers would navigate at night with the aid of bonfires strategically placed on the ground. During the day, oversized concrete arrows were placed on the ground, pointing the way. Introduction of radio navigational aids meant that pilots could fly without seeing landmarks on the ground. They navigated at higher altitudes, through and over clouds. Finally, navigation was made even easier and more efficient with transmitted radio waves in the aircraft. Most pilots utilize GPS today. (Obviously, a plane's GPS is much more intricate than the ones we rely on!). They must have faith in things that they are not able to see.

Your navigation through life is similar. Sometimes you can glide along, using beautiful scenery and landmarks to help you navigate to the next destination. There is no turbulence, only clear views, so the ride is smooth and peaceful. Happy times surround you. Friendly people are nearby passengers. Everyone is fed, comfortable, and happy.

Some trips in your lives, however, are not pleasant. You don't even want to arrive at a destination. You just want to get off the plane right now. You don't want to be on this ride! Cancer, heart attack, death of a child, depression, fire, budgets, hurricane, divorce, injury, being laid off bring the peaceful ride to a dark, scary, treacherous ride instead. During these times, you need to reach for the navigation system that you already have set up. You will be able to maneuver past paralyzing emotions and fears without sight. God is and always will be your pilot, whether the flight is smooth or turbulent.

If the ride is an enjoyable one, thanks and appreciation for the pilot is often forgotten or taken for granted. He is indeed the pilot. An inaccurate picture may lead you to believe that you have the controls and that the positive ride is somehow related to your strength or maneuvering. That picture is a fallacy.

God is your pilot when the ride is smooth. God is your pilot when questions are unanswered. God is your pilot when your heart is broken. God is your pilot when you can't see the next step. God is your pilot when all the other navigation devices have failed. God is the pilot all the time.

Yes, your decision was guided to board and fly on this plane— the Pilot never forced your hand. But God has promised, He will be your Pilot until the very end.

> Being confident of this, that He who began a good
> work in you will carry it on to completion until
> the day of Christ Jesus. (Philippians 1:6, NIV)

But then the darkness comes. While facing fear or uncertainty, finding strength can be hard and exhausting. Emotional hardships can be as devastating as physical hardships. Divorce, family issues, depression can make you feel like you have indeed been hit by a freight train. Emotional pain in the body is very heavy and real. Emotions range from torn, jagged pain to anger, bitterness, disappointment, and failure.

Faith surprisingly grows when Christians step out of the comfortable boat onto crashing waves of the scary and unknown.

Sometimes, you may feel God prompting you to walk in His plan. Bill Hybels wrote a book about how God whispers, and Hybels questions whether you truly have the guts to listen. As a Christian, you need strength from God to continue on your walk when the step ahead is dark. Heartache and pain may cause you to fear the dark.

At other times, life seems to be going along okay. No major tragedy has occurred recently. However, God is nudging you to step out and walk into a dark and anxious place. Stepping out is not limited to performing missionary work. Stepping out can take place at your home, church, or job.

Sometimes the negative voice will remind you that you are ordinary and not charismatic material, like the late Billy Graham. Why would God want to involve you? That negative voice tempts you into viewing and appreciating your slow, calm life. Why would you ever want to rock that boat?

It's during these times of nudging that faith grows. If you are reading this book, perhaps God is whispering to you. Survey the level your faith is on. If God is nudging, He may want you to take the step up to the next level of your faith. You may view yourself as a devout Christian. You truly believe in the important doctrines of your walk with God. You pray. You give. You help.

Have you grown recently in your Christian walk? Are you feeling that you are in a comfortable yet stagnant faith walk? Perhaps God is nudging you to step out and bring your faith walk to a new level.

Open your mind to new learning channels. Let God take you into a new level of your faith. Perhaps you will experience something life-changing where you won't be "in Kansas anymore." The Bible gives many verses that speak about God's everlasting protection in unknown, turbulent waters.

So here you are. You're at the point in your faith, realizing that your life path needs to intersect with God's Word. You've read the stories, verses, talked to God daily, and included Him in all aspects of your life. The questioning is always about your own attributes and not about who God is. You are a firm believer in God, just uncertain in beliefs about yourself. Your Christian playing field is solid. Why then does God seem silent at times?

Questioning begins to flow, and you are left wondering if you are asking for something that is not in God's will. The basic truth is that God will is not clear to anyone without clarification from God Himself.

Prayers are based on thoughts, emotions, and perceptions. At times, the requests do not fall within God's will, at least for that moment. God's answers are either yes, no, or not now.

Joni Eareckson Tada was seventeen years old when she suffered a spinal cord injury. During a swimming trip with her sister, Joni dove into shallow water. She is paralyzed from her neck down. Joni talks about how desperate she felt when facing the life that she was going to have to lead. God gave her hope and reassurance.

"For I know the plans I have for you," declares the Lord, "plans to prosper you and not to harm you, plans to give you hope and a future." (Jeremiah 29:11)

God's plan for Joni was to use the handicap to touch many others in Him. She not only touches those who are handicapped but others who are tempted to give up and not step forward. The purpose of Joni's life on earth is to mirror faith and determination and patience.

Continue praying for healing for those who need it. However, include God's will to your prayer. If healing is within God's will, He will make it happen! While praying, are you truly believing with confidence that healing will happen if it is God's will? Or are you haphazardly praying? You pray for healing. However, while looking at the impossible outcome, do your thoughts focus on survival methods that you will use when the darkness happens.

Have the taut faith that God can accomplish the impossible. At least six different verses talk about Jesus healing someone because their faith has made them well. A bleeding woman, a blind man, and a leper were healed because of their faith. A paralyzed servant was healed because of the faith of his centurion boss.

The first reminder is to gauge your trust level in God. Be honest. Are you setting yourself up for a negative prayer answer because you are heavily weighing in on the reality factor over a miracle? God goes above and beyond the reality factor. These are miracles. *Webster's Student Dictionary* states that the meaning of *miracle* is "an extraordinary event taken as a sign of the supernatural power of God." The bottom line is to have belief in your heart that God is able to surpass the reality of an expected outcome. Nothing is impossible for God.

Be mindful, continually, for God's will to be surrounding your prayer requests. Early in life, lessons of friendship are taught. As a friend, perform any favor possible that would lead to the happiness and well- being of a friend.

Christians feel the same rules should apply to their prayers. Since God is able to help to erase grief, suffering, or devastation, worthy prayers for funding churches or missions should be answered. So where is He? Why aren't prayers being answered?

No matter how old you become, continually remind yourself of the *need* mind-set of children. When praying, the prayer scale easily weighs down on the *self side* for wanting, needing, and deserving. You argue that God should grant your request. You continue to argue. The Bible tells you so!

> Ask and it will be given to you; seek and you will find; knock and the door will be opened to you. For everyone who asks receives; the one who seeks finds; and to the one who knocks, the door will be opened. (Matthew 7:7–8, NIV)

Parents are well-acquainted with the *must-have* approach that children try. Sometimes a child's request receives a response, and other times it does not. Christians often overlook the fact that the request lifted to God is coming from the child within, thinking that you know what's best. After all, you are the adult! Wrong! How many times have you prayed for something that, in the long run, were glad that the ending was different from what you'd hoped?

Continue to ask according to His will. The silence that you feel may be God's way of letting you know that your request needs more evaluation. Perhaps God has already provided whatever you are asking for, and you just don't see it yet. Either way, God's plan will be completed in the end.

> Being confident of this, that he who began a good work in you will carry it on to completion until the day of Christ Jesus. (Philippians 1:6, NIV)

God provides the essentials needed.

> Now may the God of peace who brought again from the dead our Lord Jesus, the great shepherd of the sheep, by the blood of the eternal covenant,

> equip you with everything good that you may do
> his will, working in us that which is pleasing in his
> sight, through Jesus Christ, to whom be the glory
> forever and ever. Amen. (Hebrews 13:20–21, ESV)

Did God forget? (Forgetting is something that I would find familiar. Honest truth? I am forgetting things all the time. I forget where my car is parked, tasks on my to-do list, peoples' names and where I know them from. Someone may ask if there are memories of an event happening while there. Truthfully? I may not remember being there in the first place!)

Some peoples remember everything. They can even state what the weather pattern was at a certain time in the past. People with memories like that may never consider the thought of God forgetting them because forgetting anything or anyone is not familiar to them.

However, some with short-term-memory issues may find themselves questioning God often in this area. How can God be omniscient, seeing and knowing all and remembering every detail?

God, are You there? Are You listening? Can You hear? Did You forget?

David, whose strength and courage defeated the huge enemy Goliath, had similar questions when God wasn't answering him.

> How long, Lord? Will you forget me forever?
> How long will you hide your face from me? How
> long must I wrestle with my thoughts and day
> after day have sorrow in my heart? (Psalm 13:1–2)

To never be forgotten seems like an impossible feat. God cherishes you. God provides the truths in the Bible to tell us how He feels. Here are two such reminders of these truths:

> Are not two sparrows sold for a cent? And yet not
> one of them will fall to the ground apart from
> your Father. But the very hairs of your head are

all numbered. So do not fear; you are more valuable than many sparrows. (Matthew 10:29–31)

See, I have engraved you on the palms of my
hands; your walls are ever before me. (Isaiah
49:16, NIV)

React in a similar way to concepts such as electricity and technology. You may not understand all of the working parts you have
enough experiences to know that it works!

When all you hear is silence, another question often asked is
whether or not the silence is a result of a sin. Are you being punished?

How long will my enemy triumph over me?
Look on me and answer, Lord my God.
Give light to my eyes, or I will sleep in death,
And my enemy will say, "I have overcome him,"
And my foes will rejoice when I fall.
But I trust in your unfailing love;
My heart rejoices in your salvation.
(Psalm 13:3–5)

Chapter 28

Why is God Silent?

G od does not punish you by making bad things happen to you. If some calamity happens unexpectedly in your life, it's never a payback for whatever sin you may have committed. God is good, through and through. Jesus took the place of any paybacks. However, the realization throughout the whole journey of this book is that blatant honesty with yourself is the key. Are you praying to God about forgiveness for a sin that, in truth, you are not ready to move away from? It's similar to receiving a meaningless apology from someone who is not truly feeling remorse but is being forced to say the words.

Are you truly sorry for this action and desperately want to remove it from your life? Are you truly willing to take painful steps to remove yourself from its clutches so that this sin will not reoccur?

God cannot be fooled with false playacting. Perhaps His silence is His way of telling you that when you are ready to be honest and talk, He will be there.

Jesus felt the sad feeling of God's silence and felt neglected and forgotten during His own crucifixion. Did God truly turn away from His only Son?

> And at three in the afternoon Jesus cried out in a
> loud voice, "Eloi, Eloi, lema sabachthani?" means
> "My God, my God, why have you forsaken me?"
> (Mark 15:34, Matthew 27:46)

My God, My God, why hast Thou forsaken Me?
(Psalm 22:1)

Many Bible experts say that for that short time, Jesus was separated from God because He was substituting himself for our sins.
God, being Holy and merciful, *turned His back on sin*. This was an
excruciating time for Jesus. Not only did he have the physical anguish
of being crucified but also the mental anguish of separation from the
Father. This was the first and only time He was ever separated from His
Father. This was the only record of Jesus not calling God His Father.

For those dark moments when Jesus was overladen with all
our sins, God could not be part of sin. God did not turn His back
and permanently reject His Son. We know that Jesus is seated at the
right hand of His Father. For the time of the crucifixion, God didn't
answer Jesus, but He never stopped loving Him.

Historians say that Martin Luther is said to have gone into
seclusion for a long time trying to understand this concept. He came
away as confused as when he began.

> For my thoughts are not your thoughts, neither
> are your ways my ways," declares the Lord. "As
> the heavens are higher than the earth, so are my
> ways higher than your way and my thoughts than
> your thoughts. (Isaiah 55: 8–9, NIV)

No matter how many times the crucifixion is studied, your
minds (even the Einstein minds!) can't wrap around it. Faith in God's
character and the love of God has to be relied on. God would never
give up or turn His back on us. No matter how terrible the sin that
was committed, because of Jesus, if truly sorry, forgiveness will be
granted. Strong reminders of this are found in the Bible:

> Be strong and courageous. Do not be afraid or
> terrified because of them, for the LORD your God
> goes with you; he will never leave you nor forsake
> you. (Deuteronomy 31:6, NIV)

There are times when you really feel like you need to hear from God. Other times, perhaps praying while riding a metro to work, you graciously accept and expect that God is not talking back at that moment and answering your prayer. However, there are occurrences that happen in your life that you are begging God to answer.

Emotional pain or anxiety can attack like a bullet or come on like a nagging headache that will not go away. Sudden/traumatic events cause us to cry out to God for ASAP help! A sudden death, losing a child or best friend, being fired, bad news, family drama, crime, failure of a big project are these 911 times in our lives.

You also cry out to God over chronic, persistent problems. These anxieties are topics of many talks with God because they continue to cause upheavals in your life. Perhaps they lie dormant in between upheavals, but the problems will not go away. Troubled family members, finances, chronic illnesses, divorces, addictions, rejections, poor life decisions fall under the chronic and persistent category. You long to hear God's voice.

Dry spells are examples when Christians long for the need to hear from God. Every Christian—even the Bible scholars, monks, and famous evangelists—go through dry spells in their faiths. Sister Teresa spent the last fifty years of her life in almost total spiritual darkness and feeling the absence of God in her heart. Her letters and personal writings were released ten years after she died. They are included in the book *Come Be My Light: The Private Writings of the Saint of Calcutta*. Like Jesus on the cross, she wondered how long her Lord would stay away.

Sister Teresa had been living the life of a Loreto sister for twenty years. Her days were spent praying, meditating, and giving herself in service to others. Mother Teresa traced her "calling" to the date of September 10, 1946. "It was on this day," she wrote, "in the train to Darjeeling that God gave me the 'call within a call' to satiate the thirst of Jesus by serving Him in the poorest of the poor." During that train ride, Mother Teresa received a deep sense of how Jesus was thirsting for the poor, the dying, and the forgotten. He was longing for their love, and He was longing to share His love with them. So many homeless and hopeless were easy prey for temptation and sin. So many sick and dying in the slums were longing for someone to give them a cup of cool water, a word of comfort, or a gentle embrace. But no one was helping them.

Mother Teresa sensed that God was calling her to care for these poor souls, both materially and spiritually. She sensed that by giving them the attention and love they craved, she could bring Jesus to them and, in the process, quench both their thirst for Him and His thirst for them.

During this time of her initial "calling" into the slums of Calcutta at thirty-six years old, Mother Teresa felt very close to Jesus. She said she heard His voice speaking to her heart. As He unfolded His plan for her and her new order, Jesus would call her "My own spouse" and "My own little one," and she would respond by calling Him "my own Jesus." Mother Teresa was very close in step with Jesus. Her world was completely His world. The darkness didn't come until she actually began that work two years later.

Many times, when a separation is felt from God, you turn toward extra prayer, repentance for sins, and increased surrendering your life to Jesus. Often these actions turn the darkness into a spiritual growth. For Mother Teresa, this was no temporary dry spell. There was no relief given by extra prayer or asking for forgiveness. Mother Teresa experienced this silent darkness for the rest of her life. However, from her actions and conversations with the poor in the slums of Calcutta, Mother Teresa never gave into the darkness. She continued to love Jesus, believe, and trust. She never stopped surrendering to God's will, even in this darkness. She felt somehow that God Himself had planned her darkness, and she had vowed as a young nun not to refuse Jesus anything He asked of her.

Rather than leave the slums and return to the convent or give up on the church completely, Mother Teresa pressed on.

About eleven years working in the slums, Mother Teresa confided in another spiritual director. After this guidance and counsel, she came to understand what was going on in her. Mother Teresa's response was, "I have come to love the darkness," she wrote, "for I believe now that it is a part, a very, very small part of Jesus's darkness and pain on earth." Mother Teresa showed in this letter and others that she had come to see her painful situation as a way of sharing in Jesus's life, a mysterious sharing in His suffering on the cross.

So how did Mother Teresa respond to this darkness and emptiness? For years, she grieved over it, wondering what she could possibly have done to make the Lord withdraw from her. Was there some secret sin or defect on her soul? Had she displeased him in some way? She continued her work, however, and confided about her inner turmoil to her confessor and spiritual director, both of whom helped counsel her.

A sign of her faith was to stay faithful. Rather than collapsing in despair, rather than returning to the security of the Loreto convent, rather than running away from religious life, Mother Teresa pressed on. She sensed somehow that God Himself was behind her darkness, and she had vowed as a young woman not to refuse Jesus anything He asked of her.

Why would God place such a burden on Mother Teresa? Perhaps this answer comes by looking at God's special calling. Mother Teresa traced this call to the date of September 10, 1946. "It was on this day," she wrote, "in the train to Darjeeling that God gave me the 'call within a call' to satiate the thirst of Jesus by serving Him in the poorest of the poor." During that train ride, Mother Teresa received a deep sense of how Jesus was thirsting for the poor, the dying, and the forgotten. He was longing for their love, and He was longing to share His love with them. So many homeless and hopeless were easy prey for temptation and sin. So many sick and dying in the slums were longing for someone to give them a cup of cool water, a word of comfort, or a gentle embrace. But no one was helping them.

Mother Teresa sensed that God was calling her to care for these poor souls, both materially and spiritually. She sensed that by giving them the attention and love they craved, she could bring Jesus to them and, in the process, quench both their thirst for Him and His thirst for them. And she sensed that this calling would cost her quite a bit. It seems, however, that she was not expecting the cost to be as steep as it really was.

Not only would she bear the cost of actually experiencing the poverty of those she cared for; God wanted her to feel spiritually poor as well. And so He withdrew from her so that she could meet these abandoned people as one of them. She felt their feelings of being isolated, lonely, and forgotten. God remained *distant* from Mother Teresa so that she could truly feel the desire for love and acceptance that these poor people wished for. God made it feel as if He was rejecting her so that she could understand how alienated and isolated the poor people felt.

In this union with the poor, Mother Teresa came to understand and experience herself the thirst that Jesus has for all. Imagine being able to visually see someone whom you desire to talk to but not being able to communicate. That is how Jesus feels with someone who doesn't know Him.

Imagine your feelings if you trusted and spent time talking to a best friend, and suddenly that friend rejected you. That is how Mother Teresa felt.

Perhaps you may not be an avid biblical scholars or a Mother Teresa. However, every Christian has faced stretches of uncertain stillness from God. If your heart is in the right place, walking in God's will, you must trust God's almighty power to keep stepping forward in the silence and darkness. You may not be sure that this is God's *calling* like Mother Teresa, but you will know when walking in the truth. Thankfully, God knows that the thought process is simple and confusing. He will lead you in the direction that He wants you to go. He will provide you with the wisdom and clarity that this is the wrong direction even though your heart is not sure.

Mother Teresa's example shows us the importance of saturating your days with God's Spirit, even while traveling on a train. Be prepared. God may speak to you about a specific area that He wants your service to be centered on. Confide in special prayer and faith guides. Pastors, teachers, and respected friends serve as spiritual guides. These guides may be used by God to give you messages even when God Himself seems quiet.

Mother Teresa did not hear from God, even after her talks with her spiritual guide. The guide gave her the understanding that this dark silence was indeed God's plan. God wanted to help Mother Teresa to truly experience and understand what these people were feeling.

When you feel like God is silent when you feel like you are walking in His plan, try to step outside of your emotions. God may be teaching lessons just by acting silently at this time. There are many reasons that God may have for teaching these lessons by seeming silent. Perhaps He wants to see how deep your faith really is. It's easy to have faith in something that is visible. The question is how deeply will you trust in His Word when you cannot feel or see it?

Perhaps by seeming silent, He is working His plan for someone else. God uses Christians as examples to others. You may never know what His intentions are. Mother Teresa may not have been alive still, but reading her thoughts and prayers touched someone's life. Perhaps like Mother Teresa, God wants you to feel the emotions of people who feel deserted or forgotten.

God's ways are not your ways! He has good reasons for whatever He is doing. You may not know the facts, but you have to trust Him.

CHAPTER 29

WHY IS THIS HAPPENING TO ME?

E ven when you make all the necessary preparations for a smooth ride, there are times when bad things happen. You may experience an accident, or your car breaks down. God remains with you, and in spite of the anguish and questioning, God still holds the plan. You find yourself questioning God because you can't see the whole picture.

Some friends enjoy doing puzzles. Leisurely sitting around the unfinished puzzle, enjoying it, and knowing or hoping that when they return to meander through it again, the puzzle will be exactly the way it was left.

My sister, a true puzzle lover, has a special table set up with whatever puzzle she is working on at the time. You can't be in the room for a gathering at her house and not look at the picture on the puzzle box and try to find a piece to fit. It's human nature with puzzles!

Working in this fashion on a puzzle can feel lot like your life feels during a happy time. You enjoy visualizing the finished picture, moving pieces around at your leisure, and trusting that when you come back to enjoy it, pieces will be intact and ready to move at your command.

But sometimes a devastating crisis happens in your life. The beautiful puzzle life is nothing as you had hoped it would be. It could be a sudden death of someone close, a debilitating illness, accident, or financial peril like loss of a job or house.

Years ago, as a Christmas present joke (being the caring and loving sister I am), I gave my sister a beautiful puzzle. But here's the clincher: I took the pieces out of the box and gave them to her with no picture to look at. Sometimes, much to our chagrin, life can be like the puzzle with no box. The magnitude of the crisis hits, and suddenly you can't see the completed picture of your life.

You've always believed in the goodness of God and that He has a map of special plans made out for your life. You've made good choices and are a remarkably decent person. Thanking Him for blessings comes naturally. But when tragedy or anguish hits, you falter. Why this, God? Why? Why? Why? You do not understand!

Your body is riddled with heartbreak, pain, and debilitating fears. There is no strength or desire to take another step and go on. Anger and resentment boil, and the target is God Himself. You don't deserve to be in this state at all. You cannot understand! You wish that you felt the peace and strength to believe that God's words were written for you.

> And we know that in all things God works for
> the good of those who love him, who have been
> called according to his purpose. (Romans 8:28)

Peace and strength to listen and believe? Resentful feelings block the way.

Listen. God is speaking. In the middle of your anguish, He is speaking. He speaks to you when you are quietly praying, crying, fixing breakfast, shopping, working, walking, or driving. God is your Best Friend, your Counselor, your Advisor, your Technician, your Teacher, and your Protector. He holds the key to every door that needs to open. He hears every emotion, even during moments when life seems too painful to talk about. God is willing to bring hope and happiness back, even when the pieces seem hopeless and askew. He will work for your good because you have been called to His purpose, one surface at a time.

Even after the devastating crisis has passed, many times you are caught in the tailspin and still don't hear God's voice. The focus is still on the past crisis, and the ears are not listening. It's like suffering from hearing loss, owning the hearing aids, but turning them off.

God will speak to you in multiple ways. Now you need to learn how to identify His voice and begin listening to what He wishes to tell you.

God speaks through other people all the time. He puts thoughts of you on someone's heart. Maybe you are struggling with family members. Maybe you are experiencing an illness or losing a job. Maybe you are facing stress at work. Maybe you feel lonely or unappreciated. Maybe you lost the love of your life. Maybe there is a problem that no one knows about, and you feel alone and can't talk to anyone. Maybe you just want to know that it's going to be okay.

He speaks through others. You may not even realize that it is God who is speaking through someone else's words.

A phone call from a friend, a handwritten card telling you that God put you on that person's heart, a person on a radio channel that says exactly what you needed to hear. The words of a song being played describes your feelings exactly. You refer to these moments as coincidences instead of *God* incidences.

Does God always hold up traffic, use a loud voice, and remind you to listen? No. A vital component needed in improving your faith walk is to start being in tune to God's presence in your life all the time. How do you make this happen?

Start early in the morning before your feet ever hit the floor.

A simple prayer to start the day is asking God to please show you the ways He is working in your life on that day. Ask Him to make it very clear to you, helping you to willingly do your part and to remind you throughout the day to look and listen.

The next step is to open your eyes and look beyond your tunnel vision at the world around. Look at the trees, flowers, and stars. Listen to the sounds of the birds, the pastor, crickets, and musical notes. Look at and listen to the people who interact with you throughout the day. Family, neighbors, friends, and strangers may have something to pass on to you. Be mindful that God speaks and acts through many different people in the course of your day. You don't want to miss it!

CHAPTER 30

STEP OUT OF YOUR COMFORT ZONE

Y ou've been praying more regularly, not as diligently or frequently as you desire, but regularly. Prayer time has improved and faith walk, as a whole, is much healthier than the state where you found yourself before. Talking with God has changed your mind about your significance in God's eyes.

Perspective on life has been modified a great deal. You even find yourself asking God more frequently to show you His direction. Now you're ready to listen.

Thoughts of a mission field are usually coupled with amazing missionaries and families who sacrifice safe and standard lives for harsh, unsafe, poverty-stricken conditions. Other mission fields are right in front of Christians who are blinded to them. That blindness comes because these missions are familiar with other visible *missionaries* handling them.

My three dogs love to run. We live in a completely fenced-in third of an acre, so their time is spent outside most of the time. The majority of the time, they meander around the yard, running occasionally, if a stranger comes close to the fence. However, there is a park a short distance from the house. When the dogs visit the park, they are excited and never stop running. The adventure is evident. The smells and environment are not the familiar land that they are used to.

Churches are similar to homes and yards. The smells and people are the familiar ones you are accustomed to. You meander, but do not excitedly run from place to place. Look outside of your church doors into the mission fields that are right in front. Start by having these mission fields available for guests at your own church. Some mission fields are Alcoholic Anonymous meetings, Narcotics Anonymous, Gamblers Anonymous, single parents, sex-addiction meetings, pregnancy centers, soup kitchens, thrift stores, food banks. They are viewed as good and helpful causes but not mission fields.

As true and faithful Christians, if called personally by God to spend three hours in a mission field working on a specific project, most would do it. But there are many negative thoughts that hold volunteers back. Your personality is not outgoing or evangelistic, and that type of activity makes you uncomfortable.

Jesus didn't gather people to Himself to speak to them in scholarly upper tones that could only be understood by Pharisees and Sadducees and well-educated people. Jesus met people where they were in life: problems and dirtiness and rejections. Sometimes churches are not inviting places to those in need.

With all the crime and fear in the nation right now, it's naturally easy to be filled with feelings of distrust. Look deeply within yourself. Do you have inner qualms about having unkempt, scraggly-looking people in your church environment?

> So from now on we regard no one from a worldly
> point of view. Though we once regarded Christ in
> this way, we do so no longer. (2 Corinthians 5:16)

Churches need to provide a welcoming purpose for people of all levels of life to come to church. Members do not have to be evangelists, cramming Bible verses down a visitor's throat. If your church can provide security measures within your building that keeps your level of fear or suspicion down, that is a wonderful asset.

Being a mission volunteer doesn't mean you are required to lead meetings. Most of the outside meetings like AA and NA already have a facilitator in place. They are merely looking for a meeting place.

Your jobs as missionaries in this mission field may just be a presence in the church building while this meeting is taking place. Fears and anxieties pop up. Perhaps expectations may be to tie down a permanent commitment, and your time is limited. God will move in you during those moments you give to His mission field.

> And whether you turn to the right or turn to the left, your ears will hear a message behind you: "This is the way, walk in it." (Isaiah 30:21)

Give God the best service you are able, even if it's a onetime sacrifice. If He is leading you to make a more regular commitment, you'll feel the tug within. You will have a feeling of completeness wash through you after the decision is made.

The emptiness that you didn't even know existed in your heart will fill in spite of any obstacles: finances, time restraints, and opposition. Just to review an earlier chapter, if this mission is something that God wishes you to do in His kingdom, you are surely going to run across opposition of some kind as Satan tries to deter you.

After replanting a sweet-potato vine in the summer, the leaves were droopy and forlorn looking. Many times, during those days, the thoughts came about throwing it away or moving it out of eyesight. However, it remained. After days of looking forlorn and sad, the leaves began to perk up again. Every day, the plant got fuller and healthier.

Frequently taking on a new project or mission will make you feel tired and droopy like the sweet-potato vine. God will move within your heart if this mission is some service that He desires for you to be involved with in His kingdom. You will feel that little burst of happiness when you feel the droopiness disappear and the life coming back in yourself and your church.

Stormie O'Martien wrote a wonderful book called *Just Enough Light for the Step I'm On*. When the path ahead seems scary or uncertain, as my own life became, you have to trust God, even when the path seems dark ahead.

CHAPTER 31

FIRST CHAPTER OF THE NEXT
BEST SELLER OF MY LIFE

In closing, as you have learned that building a better life is a marathon and not a quick sprint. The finish line will be your realization of who you are and the person you strive to be. God has laid the necessary proponents for your success in this realization very clearly.

God created you, treasures you, leads you, and promises to never give up on you.

With those facts in mind, you are capable of facing every hardship, challenge, or attack from Satan. Memories from your past still can cause pain, anger, and weariness to your soul, but they don't determine the person who you can be. God is right beside you, willing to carry you when your strength is gone. God will help you find His goodness even in areas where there seems to be nothing salvageable.

Unsettling parts of your present life that tatters your sails every day can be quieted and polished in His name. You will be able to hear your Father off in the distance saying, "Well done, good and faithful servant. I'm very proud of you."

Walking in faith will bloom like daffodils in spring. Those unseemly bulbs that are planted in your faith will blossom and grow when you need them the most.

Hopefully, you've learned that it's okay to be brutally honest with yourself. No matter how dirty, torn, or ugly you may feel, *nothing* can keep you from the love and forgiveness of the Father.

God has a purpose, a plan, for your life. He will spin a beautiful quilt of your life, using all squares filled with your messes and regrets and fears. God didn't create you and then change His mind because of all the imperfections. He did not pick another for His plan. He has chosen you.

A clear road map is available through the Bible and will lead you. You have to closely listen for His cues. God sends messages through words, people, and circumstances. He is walking closely beside you and speaks often. Take out the white noise that is distracting you from hearing His messages and listen. You will hear His voice.

Never give up, no matter how hopeless your circumstances may seem. God will use that pain and challenge to build a stronger and more faithful you. Each step is leading you toward God. His promise of heaven awaits. You may not understand (or agree) with His ways, but nothing happens for naught.

All the chapters from your past, your present, and your individual walks of faith get written into God's *big* book of His chosen children's lives. The book is not yet finished.

Today is the first day of the rest of your life. How you orchestrate your book's chapters that lead up to your last chapter is completely up to you.

God will grant you clarity and clear away any confusion you encounter while you are truly seeking Him. You will try to pay attention amidst all the distractions.

So say the following prayer aloud:

> Lord. I am paying attention. I am listening. How are You going to transform me? The desire of my heart is to conform to the Christian example that You created me to be. Show me today the plans that You put in place to complete within me during the chapters of this next *best seller* of my life. I can hardly wait to see!

About the Author

O n a warm April day, within one minute, Nancie Seymour's life drastically changed.

As a preschool director, married with four children, she was living a very content, yet busy, life.

On that April day, sitting as a passenger, a speeding truck crashed into their van.

Three weeks of being unresponsive in a coma was followed by hospitalization for months, feeding tubes and wheel chair. Suffering with a traumatic brain injury, she had to re-learn how to walk, dress, speak, swallow, write, and eventually drive.

Although she couldn't speak, her voice screamed out silently inside, trying to tell others, *I'm still in here!*" For months she could only view the world in snap-shots, never able to see the whole picture at one time.

She learned firsthand, how to trust in God during that dark and hopeless time. Seemingly there was no light at the end of the tunnel. But God had other plans in mind.

On the outside today, the injuries are no longer visible. However, that former person will never return, and challenges will always exist. Running, jumping, and singing will never be possible.

God can use bad times for His good. Her hope is that, if facing a mountain ahead right now and feeling the darkness pressing in, don't give up. Step toward your future from where you are right now, and not as the person who you used to be. God has a plan for you and that will not change.

One Surface at a Time: -Moving Beyond Mediocre reminds you that although your life may be hectic, and hurried or painful, all of the keys are available, to equip you with peace, and purpose in your life.

Find shreds of hope and hold on. Whatever situation you find yourself in, God is not done with you yet.

CPSIA information can be obtained
at www.ICGtesting.com
Printed in the USA
BVHW031317261218
536450BV00001B/21/P